10/12

Home
BY NOVOGRATZ

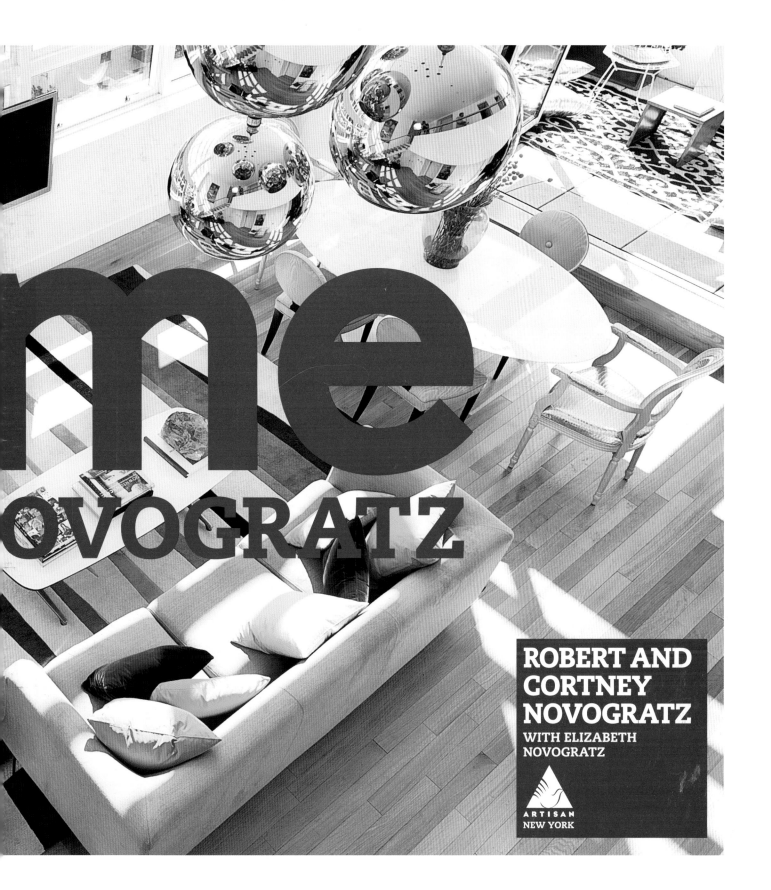

me
OVOGRATZ

ROBERT AND CORTNEY NOVOGRATZ

WITH ELIZABETH
NOVOGRATZ

ARTISAN
NEW YORK

For illustration credits, see page 320, which functions as an extension of this page.

Published by Artisan
A division of Workman Publishing Company, Inc.
225 Varick Street
New York, NY 10014-4381
artisanbooks.com

Published simultaneously in Canada by
Thomas Allen & Son, Limited

Library of Congress Cataloging-in-Publication Data
Novogratz, Robert.
Home by Novogratz / Robert and Cortney Novogratz
with Elizabeth Novogratz.
p. cm.
Includes index.
ISBN 978-1-57965-499-3
1. Interior decoration. I. Novogratz, Cortney. II. Novogratz, Elizabeth.
III. Title.
NK2110.N685 2012
747—dc23
2012012155

Design by Eight and a Half,
New York

Printed in China
First printing, September 2012

10 9 8 7 6 5 4 3 2 1

TO MOM AND POPS—

We are inspired by you every single day. You've infected us with your zest for life, your love of antiquing (whether at a suburban garage sale or the Paris flea markets), and your tireless passion for decorating and redecorating.

But, most important, you've been the role models of a lifetime: you've taught us what it means to show up no matter what, to be a family, and to love every single minute of it.

We love you.

P.S. Thanks for having such a bright and cool daughter like Elizabeth, who was a big help in writing this book.

CONTENTS

BEFORE AFTER

FOREWORD

DECORATING. It's not unlike cooking, dressing, anything that reflects one's personal sense of poetry. When it's right, it's wonderful, dreamlike, and appears oh-so-effortless—leaving those of us who may not have the skill for it in awe and, let's be honest, a wee bit frustrated. The idea of filling a space, a room, or an entire home with a sense of who you are and how you feel about the world around you can be daunting: There are so many choices and challenges, and then the dreaded expense.

Well, if it's decorating advice you need, long for, and stay up late poring over magazines for inspiration in search of, the wait is over! In this incomparable book, two ingenious designers are sharing all their clever ideas, tricks, and skills for making a space exactly what you want—but better, cooler, and within your actual budget—showing us all how to decorate and design spaces for the active lives we are living, with children, dogs, friends, and visiting out-of-towners, who sometimes stay, well, longer than expected (the risk of a too-fabulous guest room!). It's really incredible, but coming from these two it's simply no wonder. There is something special about Robert and Cortney Novogratz. They are not unlike their gift for decor: lively, happy, outspoken, and altogether unique. Everything you could ever need to renew and revive any space is right in your hands.

Go on, get to work!

—JULIA ROBERTS

BRAZIL

INTRODUCTION

Since we started designing twenty years ago, we've been traveling the globe, amassing an enormous collection of design ideas to bring back home and put to use. After more than sixty projects, we've learned that no matter where we are, there is usually something right in front of us to be inspired by, an idea to stick in our back pockets, or something that can spark our imaginations. We've learned that as long as you keep your eyes open, inspiration is everywhere: restaurants, bars, stores, hotels, magazines, websites, nature, museums, the country, the city—even your next-door neighbor's living room.

Over the past few years, we've been fortunate enough to work on projects of every variety. We've designed everything from single-family homes to retail stores to a boutique hotel, and have been challenged to come up with innovative solutions and creative techniques for hundreds of different design dilemmas. But we like to work off-the-cuff; we find that the pressure helps rather than hinders.

BROOKLYN, NEW YORK

QUEENS, NEW YORK

We've worked with every kind of budget, and more often than not it's the smaller budgets that push us to become more creative, and we love the challenge. We've taken a lot of risks—some have worked, others have failed completely—but each time we've learned something new.

There are design issues that seem to come up again and again, no matter the kind of home we are working on. Many people are paralyzed by the fear of making mistakes, especially in rentals or temporary homes, and don't know where to begin. Oftentimes people complain that they're just too busy to decorate, that they'll wait until the kids are older or the job stress lessens or they have more money. But design doesn't need to be so complicated, and the projects featured in this book were chosen to prove just that. We've selected the ones with the most takeaway ideas and broken them down into a step-by-step process to explain to you why we made the decisions we did. We hope to inspire you to use your imagination, borrow our ideas, and take more risks with your living space—whether it be painting your bedroom lime green or buying that dream fixer-upper.

Throughout this book, you'll see over and over again what a difference decluttering can make in transforming a space. Most of us have too much stuff, and we (and our homes) get lost in it. Every time we begin a project, the first thing we do is clear out the clutter. Most people have a hard time parting with their possessions, but it's an important part of the process. Even our own kids have had to learn that lesson the hard way. Years ago, a week or so before a move, we did a massive toy purging in the middle of the night. We took the bags of throwaway toys that couldn't be donated out to the curb, knowing that the garbage collectors would come before the kids were up and outside. Later that morning as we were walking our four-year-old twin daughters to preschool, one of them spotted a homeless man pushing a shopping cart filled with her discarded stuffed animals and dress-up clothes. She pointed and sobbed, "He has our toys. Those are our toys. Get our toys back!" It was an early lesson in letting go, and thankfully, she wasn't too traumatized.

We've been lucky in that our clients have been kind and extremely brave. We are grateful to all of them for allowing us into their homes—and, in most cases, letting us get rid of everything and start from scratch. We've incorporated our style, philosophy, and design concepts throughout these chapters—using bold color and big art, mixing vintage with modern and high-end with low-end—in hopes of sharing ideas and techniques with you. Mostly, though, we hope that this book will serve as a source of inspiration—a reminder that your home is a reflection of you.

Design doesn't need to be so complicated.

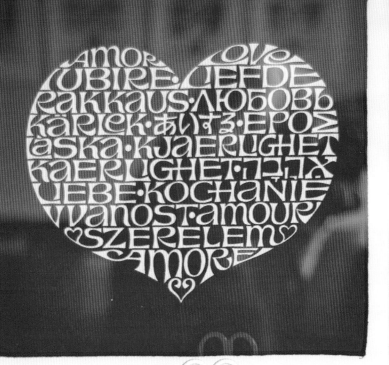

14
JANUARY

Queens Condo

Steve Koch and Susan Whitley came to us because they needed a few design solutions for their condo in Long Island City, an up-and-coming neighborhood in Queens, New York. The couple, along with their five-year-old daughter, Samantha, had moved into the two-bedroom, two-bathroom, 1,100-square-foot apartment about a year before we met them. After the initial move-in, they went to work painting and furnishing their living room, but never felt completely comfortable and struggled with how to manipulate the layout of this single room into a place that would fulfill all of their family's needs.

The apartment was in a modern building with clean lines and floor-to-ceiling windows. It had a ton of potential and just required a clever layout and storage solutions, a new paint job, fun and

WHERE WE STARTED

THE BUDGET
$40,000

THE GOAL
To create a modern, clean, multifunctional living space that included a TV and seating area, a dining area, an office, and a playroom

THE CLIENTS' WISH LIST

1. A multifunctional room
2. Storage and organization
3. A work space for Susan
4. A midcentury modern aesthetic
5. A flexible dining solution

THE PUMPKIN-COLORED WALLS MADE THE ROOM FEEL LIKE AN ORANGE BOX.

CLUTTERED FLOORS / BARE WALLS

THE ROOM
WAS
SCREAMING
FOR A FOCAL
WALL.

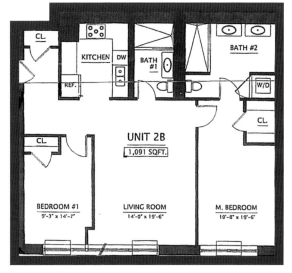

personal art on the walls, and furniture that better fit the space (and the clients' taste). The space needed to serve many functions: living room, dining room, home office, and a play area for Samantha. The challenge was to combine those needs in a single space that still had great flow.

Steve and Susan's furnishings were simple pieces that seemed temporary and utilitarian. The entire space had been painted orange, and the ceiling fixtures were the only lights.

Our plan was to flip the layout of this entire room so that we could take advantage of the longest wall for a custom storage unit. We also wanted to brighten up the space and find midcentury modern pieces that Steve and Susan would love. We enjoy projects like this one because half the work is problem solving: how to figure out better layouts and smarter ways to live.

THIS GRAY BRIGHTENS UP THE ROOM.

PICK AN IMPORTANT FAMILY PHOTO AND PUT IT ON DISPLAY.

STEP 1

REPAINT

The main room had been painted orange. It wasn't a terrible choice, but it didn't work for this space. It made the room look narrower than it was and feel dark, even when the shades were up. We repainted it light gray, and the change in color immediately made the room feel large and airy.

STEPHANIE T.

We asked Stephanie T. from Vitsoe a few questions about the 606—the shelving system we used in Steve and Susan's apartment.

Q: Tell us about Vitsoe's 606 Universal Shelving System.

A: The 606 Universal Shelving System is a modular shelving system that was designed by Dieter Rams for Vitsoe in 1960. It continues to be produced and sold by Vitsoe to this day. Shelves, cabinets, and tables are all hung from aluminum E-Tracks. These E-Tracks can be mounted directly to the wall or attached to Vitsoe's X-Posts. When the E-Tracks are attached to X-Posts, the system can stand slightly away from the wall, or it can be compressed between the floor and the ceiling to stand in the center of a room.

Q: Where is the best place in the home for the 606?

A: The 606 can really work in any room in the home. The bedroom, office, living room, or kitchen can all use the same system but in different ways—to hang clothes, display books, keep cutlery, store toys, organize AV equipment, or to work at with a computer or laptop, for example.

Q: What is the most common storage need?

A: We often plan systems for TV and media storage, work space, and file storage, and sometimes a combination of both, just like the system the Koch family now uses in their own home. Of course, there will always be the need to display books on shelves, whether it is for a small book collection at home or an expansive university library.

Q: The 606 has a modern but timeless look; how do you achieve that?

A: The 606 shelving system is a timeless product because of its lasting quality and understated design. The system can work in any environment because it is able to blend into any setting, while still being a refined object all on its own.

STEP 2

INSTALL A SHELVING SYSTEM

Susan's work space was a white cabinet against one of the living room walls. We worked with Vitsoe to create a custom storage unit that would span the entire length of this wall and have a dedicated work area for Susan and a place for the TV and media storage, along with Samantha's books and toys.

OPEN SHELVING TO DISPLAY THE ITEMS WE LOVE TO SEE

THE CAPELLINI HI PAD CHAIR IS FROM ABC CARPET AND HOME.

CLOSED STORAGE TO HIDE EVERYTHING ELSE

WE BUILT A STAND FOR SAM'S FINGER PUPPETS. IT'S OKAY TO DISPLAY YOUR KIDS' TOYS!

We worked with Vitsoe to create a custom storage unit.

x

VINTAGE
GETS A
MAKEOVER.

RECONCEIVE THE SEATING AREA

The heater underneath the windows was big and unattractive, but moving it wasn't an option. Our carpenter, Tom Baione, built the custom box to cover it up; now it blends in.

Steve and Susan are huge fans of midcentury modern, so we knew that they'd love the 1960s lounge chair. We found it at a vintage store in Massachusetts. It wasn't in great shape, so we had it reupholstered in bright blue Maharam fabric, and we think it might look better now than it did in the sixties. The vintage Lane coffee table in front of the sofa is also a great midcentury piece. It's long and narrow and fits the space perfectly. The rug beneath it is light and simple but holds the seating area together and showcases the vintage furniture.

We found two of the poufs from different vendors on Etsy. They make the space cozy and fun. Etsy is a fantastic place to look for interesting, hip home decor, and it's usually inexpensive and a great way to find items locally.

The existing window coverings were plain top-down/bottom-up shades that were the right choice for this room, but we replaced them with a nicer gray silk version, which gave the windows more texture and weight.

POUFS ADD
TEXTURE AND
CHARACTER.

THE SOFA MIGHT
NOT BE AS BIG
AS A SECTIONAL,
BUT IT IS REALLY
COMFORTABLE
AND CAN FIT THE
WHOLE FAMILY.

IT'S NEVER TOO
LATE TO GET
YOUR FIRST
COFFEE TABLE!

ASK THE EXPERT
JEFF SCHER

Brooklyn-based artist and filmmaker Jeff Scher painted the four watercolor portraits of Samantha that hang above the sofa. We asked him a few questions about his work.

Q: When did you start painting in watercolor?
A: When I was a kid, it was all I was allowed to paint with.

Q: Why do you still choose to paint in watercolor today?
A: Watercolor is the most like cinema; the most like painting with pure light. Both film and watercolor are transparent, so the white of the screen is just like the white of the paper. It has a huge impact on how you construct an image on the page. The thing that makes watercolor so luminous is the purity of the colors. Watercolors always seem alive and fresh to me because a good watercolor has the flavor of lively brushwork.

Q: What makes a good portrait?
A: You have to look for the moment that most expresses the subject's relationship to life. It's more important that the personality come through than that the portrait be overly realistic.

REDESIGN THE DINING AREA

The existing dining area consisted of a small white table with drop-down leaves and a few ghost chairs. We replaced everything with a Hans Olsen set that could be expanded to seat more than four with a hidden leaf stored inside the table. We positioned it in the middle of the space instead of against the wall, in part because of its clever, compact, round design, but also because it was such a gorgeous piece that we wanted to show it off.

INCREDIBLE DESIGN IS BOTH BEAUTIFUL AND FUNCTIONAL. THIS TABLE WAS DESIGNED AND MADE IN 1953!

THE FLOORS WERE GORGEOUS, SO WE LET THEM SHINE.

THE CHAIRS TUCK COMPLETELY INTO THE TABLE, MAKING IT EASIER TO PLACE IN THE CENTER OF THE ROOM.

SHOW OFF YOUR CHILDREN'S ART AND PICK MULTIPLE PIECES TO FRAME TOGETHER.

We replaced everything with a Hans Olsen set.

WHERE WE ENDED

By repainting the room a lighter color and installing a Vitsoe shelving unit, we were able to maximize the functionality of this space and deliver a midcentury-modern-infused room that met all of Steve and Susan's needs.

THE TV IS EXPOSED, BUT IT FITS NICELY ON THE SHELVING.

STEVE'S
SURPRISE GIFT
FOR SUSAN'S
NEW WORK
SPACE

THE SIZE OF
THE FURNISHINGS
NEEDED TO BE
IN SCALE WITH
THE SPACE.

HOW TO

COVER UNATTRACTIVE HEATERS AND AIR-CONDITIONING UNITS

Note: These instructions are for heating and AC units with vents and controls that face up toward the ceiling.

1. Purchase one sheet of ¾-inch birch veneer plywood and cut to size. You will need to cut two pieces for sides, one for the face, and one for the top. Remember when measuring and cutting your pieces to give yourself a few extra inches to make sure the box will fit over the unit.

2. Miter the edges of all of your pieces.

3. Use wood glue to attach the pieces together at the corners, and then use wood nails or screws to secure the pieces to each other.

4. Once the unit is assembled, use a plunge bit router to create slits in the front face. This allows for air circulation.

5. Buy your grill before cutting the opening. The aluminum grill that you purchase should be the same width as the AC unit. The grill gives you access to the controls and allows for the air to blow out. Use a jigsaw to make an opening in the top piece for the aluminum grill. The grill drops into the opening, and the metal lip covers your cuts. Sand any rough edges in case you ever need to lift the entire thing out. There should be an aluminum door on your grill, so that you can pop it open to access the controls.

6. Paint or wallpaper as desired, so that the box blends into the wall.

7. Slide your box over the unit.

BUDGET ANALYSIS

CONTRACTOR/INSTALLATION FEES	$3,332.50
PAINT	$156.75
FLOORING AND CARPETS	$825.00
WINDOW TREATMENTS	$1,250.97
LIGHTING	$1,890.89
CUSTOM WALL SHELVING	$10,707.80
FURNITURE	$9,817.88
FABRIC AND UPHOLSTERY	$1,520.48
ART	$1,980.21
ACCESSORIES	$3,007.00
BOOKS	$1,092.19
ELECTRONICS	$1,757.30
TOYS	$258.41
TOTAL	**$37,597.38**

TONY

CATHY

Ski Condo

Tony Hawk is the most influential skateboarder in the world and one of the coolest people alive, so we were excited when he asked us to redo his ski house on Mammoth Mountain in California. The house was built in the early 1970s and has been Tony's vacation home for many years. He and his partner, Cathy Goodman, along with their children, spend quite a bit of time there. But when the family goes to Mammoth, they go to snowboard and kick back, not to shop, decorate, or worry about paint colors. That's where we came in.

The exterior of the house is your typical A-frame ski cabin and is similar to others nearby, but the interior looked like it hadn't been touched since the place was first built. The floors were

WHERE WE STARTED

THE GOAL
To create a hip but cozy multifunctional family vacation home

THE BUDGET
$50,000

THE CLIENT'S WISH LIST

1. A boutique hotel vibe
2. A kid-friendly and fun space
3. Durable flooring
4. Comfortable furniture
5. A great dining area for family meals

HOUSTON, WE HAVE KNOTTY PINE. EVERYWHERE.

AVOCADO IS GREAT FOR GUACAMOLE. NOT FOR THESE WALLS.

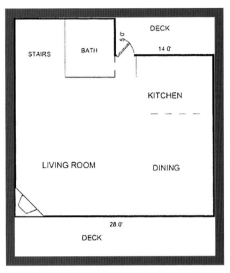

STAIRS

BATH

5 0'

DECK

14 0'

KITCHEN

LIVING ROOM

DINING

28 0'

DECK

THIS TABLE WAS BIG, BUT IT DIDN'T MAKE A STATEMENT.

covered in beige wall-to-wall carpeting, the walls were painted a drab avocado green, and the furniture was outdated, oversized, and anything but what you'd find in a boutique hotel. Most of the furniture had come from Tony's other homes, his own hand-me-downs. There was a pellet stove recessed into the original stone fireplace, which made the place feel especially dated, and the window frames and ceiling were a yellowy pine. The house needed a total overhaul.

Our goal was to make the space as hip and cool as Tony and to add design details that the whole family would enjoy. We also aimed to incorporate the spirit of Mammoth, which still has an old-school feel. Ski houses should be durable and easy, but that is no reason to forgo style.

Our first task was to clean the place out. We stripped it bare, leaving almost nothing in our wake. The furniture went first; next we ripped out the carpets. The place felt four times the size and much more open.

NARROW WOODEN LOGS (AROUND 6 INCHES IN DIAMETER) WERE USED TO CREATE THE WOODEN DISKS OF THE FACADE.

STEP1

BRING OUT THE ORIGINAL FIREPLACE

The black metal pellet stove was unattractive and looked like it had been there for a very long time. We pulled it out and exposed the open fireplace behind it. We then transformed the fireplace into the room's focal point by creating the log wall that covers the surfaces of the fireplace all the way to the ceiling.

The centerpiece of the log wall is a hand-painted animal skull that we found at City Foundry in Brooklyn. The shelves hold brightly colored toys, books, and magazines. Because the weather was still fairly warm, we filled the fireplace with a ton of candles instead of an actual fire.

FROM BROOKLYN

FIREPLACE AFTER

CANDLES ALWAYS LOOK ELEGANT AND MAKE A GREAT ADDITION FOR PARTIES.

We transformed the fireplace into the room's focal point.

FIREPLACE BEFORE

MAKE 3-D WALL ART OUT OF YOUR COLLECTIONS.

WE LOVE KNOTTY PINE (PAINTED WHITE).

THE MAIN BEAMS REMAINED AS IS TO RETAIN THE SKI-LODGE FEEL.

WE PAINTED THIS TREE TRUNK A HIGH-GLOSS SILVER AND HAD AN INSTANT SIDE TABLE.

STEP 2

REDO THE WALLS AND CEILING

The green walls and pine detailing made everything in the room feel heavy and dated. We repainted all of the walls (except the ski wall) pale blue and the trim and ceiling white. Immediately, the space felt more modern. The vaulted ceiling sets the tone for the cabin, and by painting the pine planks white, we opened up the entire room.

We replaced the miniblinds with simple roman shades on the smaller window and sheers and wool drapery on the large floor-to-ceiling windows that make up the entire back wall. The long wall of wool drapes with the sheers makes a dramatic difference. The sheers still let in a lot of light, while the continuous drapery downplays the irregularly spaced windows and doors they are hiding.

COZY UP
THE TV AREA

After we painted everything in our updated color palette, it was important to bring in a mix of textured elements to make the space feel warm after a day spent out in the cold.

We replaced the heavy, overstuffed couch and chaise longue with a sleek gray sofa from CB2 that was deep and comfortable with a clean silhouette, and two vintage chairs that we had lacquered and reupholstered in New York. Bold and colorful pillows brighten up the couch, and the marble-topped coffee table is sleek.

The TV console is made from a slab of wood that we found at a local lumberyard. It's a rustic touch against the chic color palette, and it's also a great way to showcase the toys and games.

THE TOYS ARE AN ELEMENT OF THE DECOR, ADDING CHARACTER AND COLOR.

Bring in a mix of textured elements.

DECORATE THE DINING AREA

We found the spectacular dining table at Poesis Design in Connecticut. It's high-end, but we paired it with mostly inexpensive seating to offset the cost. The eight brushed-nickel chairs are from CB2, and the faux-fur throws from Ikea soften them and make them perfect for cozying up. The suede high-back chairs at the ends of the table are from Z Gallerie and provide a great contrast.

The chandelier suspended in the room was designed by Ingo Maurer and is comprised of thin wire cables with clips on the ends that radiate out from the center. The original comes with love letters in different languages printed on paper. We love this idea, but not as much as we love personal touches, so we replaced the letters with family photos and the kids' art for a one-of-a-kind fixture.

USE A FAUX-FUR THROW TO SOFTEN METAL FURNITURE.

ASK THE EXPERT
ROB BRISTOW

Rob Bristow, one of the owners of Poesis Design, gave us his thoughts on what makes a great dining table.

Q: Tell us about your dining table philosophy.

A: As a designer, I think of dining tables as pieces of architecture, places that serve as the stage and backdrop for the moments of our lives. Each should be a place for a lazy cup of coffee, a heated discussion, or a wild table-dancing party; a place to fill out a college application. It should arouse all your senses: you should be able to hear it when you pound your fist on it, or feel it when you stroke its contours like you would a dog. Its surface should be so smooth you want to lick it. It should smell of wood and time. And when you see it, you should see history. My favorite table of all time, the inspiration for all my tables, is an incredibly long, narrow farm table in a back dining room at The Old Inn on the Green in New Marlborough, Massachusetts. The marks on its surface speak of its history. It is long enough for many, but narrow enough to encourage intimacy. It is happy full or empty.

A PERSONALIZED CHANDELIER

DISPLAYING FRESH
FRUIT = GREAT
COLOR AND
HEALTHY SNACKS

We cleared out
most of the clutter
from the shelves.

LESS IS
ALWAYS MORE
IN A SMALL
KITCHEN.

STEP 5

SPICE UP THE KITCHEN

Redoing the kitchen was not in the budget, so we mostly left it as
it was. But by scrubbing it clean and styling the countertops and
shelves, we transformed it for almost no money. We switched out
all of the knobs for more modern hardware, and the bar stools were
replaced with purple vintage stools, which brought color to the bar.
We cleared out most of the clutter from the shelves and replaced it
with a few simple design elements. The three small trees outside
the kitchen window bring life into the room.

WHERE WE ENDED

How do you transform a dull and dated space into a bright, bold, super-chic ski house? Open it up by painting the walls and ceiling, getting rid of heavy furnishings, replacing the window treatments, and adding great pops of color.

PALE-BLUE WALLS AND A WHITE CEILING FEEL CLEAN AND FRESH.

BAR STOOLS ARE A GREAT PLACE FOR UNEXPECTED POPS OF COLOR.

DRAPERY ADDS
A TOUCH
OF ELEGANCE.

SHEERS
LET THE
LIGHT IN.

CARPET-TILE
FLOORS ARE
DURABLE ENOUGH
FOR SKI AND
SNOWBOARD BOOTS.

HOW TO

BUILD A LOG WALL FIREPLACE

CONCEAL THE OLD SURROUND
Cover the three faces of the fireplace with a plywood base (we stained the base dark brown).

BUILD SHELVES
Decide how many shelves you want and how large or small the shelves will be, and build the boxes.

MOUNT THE SHELVES
Attach the boxes to the wall. Ours are recessed into the wall so that the front face is flush with the log detailing.

APPLY THE FACING
Apply the logs to the facing, covering the surface around the boxes using an adhesive (Liquid Nails), and then secure it in place using a nail gun.

USE VINTAGE TOYS AS DESIGN ELEMENTS

- Old toys and games brighten up dead spaces and bring charm to almost any type of shelf.

- Vintage wooden or metal games add character and nostalgia.

- Vinyl always looks cool.

- Robots rule.

- The best games are the old-school type that the whole family can enjoy, especially in a vacation house (leave the video games at home).

BUILD A FOCAL WALL WITH OBJECTS

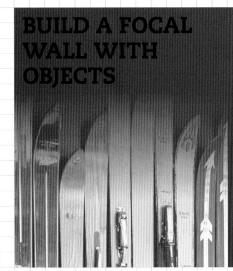

PICK A FOCAL WALL
Smaller walls are usually better. Choose a wall without windows.

COLLECT YOUR OBJECTS
Our favorite places to look for vintage objects (whatever you choose to make a wall of) are eBay and Etsy, flea markets, vintage stores, and garage sales.

PREPARE THE WALL
Paint the wall a background color that will showcase your collection.

CREATE A LAYOUT
Lay out and work through your display on the floor first to get an idea of what it will look like.

MOUNT THE OBJECTS
Attach the objects to the wall. For the ski wall, we took the screws out of the skis and put new screws straight through the skis into the wall.

BUDGET ANALYSIS

CONTRACTOR FEES	$16,000.00
PAINT	GIFT
FLOORING AND CARPETS	$4,227.18
WINDOW TREATMENTS	$4,222.00
LIGHTING	$1,220.00
FURNITURE	$17,640.00
THROWS AND PILLOWS	$1,910.00
ART	$1,057.50
HOME ACCESSORIES	$3,497.58
KITCHEN ACCESSORIES	$205.44
TOYS AND GAMES	$588.97
ELECTRONICS	$498.00
TOTAL	$51,066.67

CANDLES CAN
BE USED
AS OVERHEAD
LIGHTING.

TALL CHAIRS
LOOK GOOD
MIXED WITH
ROUND ONES.

COUNTRY
IN THE CITY

Urban Sanctuary

We met Emmy Award–winning producer David Perler in the fall of 2011 when he asked us to redo his 900-square-foot apartment in the historic Gramercy Park neighborhood of New York City. It was a charming one-bedroom, one-bathroom home in a cool prewar building. The space had a ton of character, but the kitchen was a tiny galley space that is typical in old Manhattan apartments, and the bathroom was small and cramped. Both needed to be gutted and redone, and the rest of the space needed to be opened up and decorated.

David has great taste and most of his furniture and decorative pieces were fantastic flea-market finds and vintage items he's collected over the years. While he had a lot for us to work with, we aimed to add a few modern elements, furniture that better fit the

WHERE WE STARTED

THE BUDGET
$110,000

THE GOAL
To open up a small New York City apartment and create a cozy home with an industrial feel

THE CLIENT'S WISH LIST

1. A new industrial kitchen open to the living room
2. An updated bathroom
3. A backyard makeover
4. New clothing storage
5. The Novogratz design touch

TOO MUCH ON THE FLOOR

NOT
ENOUGH
ON THE
WALLS

WHERE IS
THE COLOR?

Built-in Storage

Bathroom   Closet

Access to Patio

Entryway

Bedroom   Kitchen   Living Area

space, some art on the walls, and new lighting. He asked for pops of color throughout, but nothing too bold or crazy. And although it was a gut renovation, the space had great bones and we saved all the detailing, because that was what made this home so special.

David also had a private backyard off the living room that needed a fun but inexpensive makeover so that he could entertain friends and spend time outside.

Because of the renovations, we had a good-sized budget to work with. Redoing the kitchen and bathroom, as well as adding storage to the bedroom, would increase the value of the apartment significantly, so it was a great investment in this home.

GUT THE KITCHEN

The kitchen was a small rectangular box with very little storage or work space. By tearing down the wall between the kitchen and the living room, we opened up both spaces and made them much larger and more functional.

Inexpensive white Ikea cabinets outfitted with high-end hardware give the space a clean, finished look. The existing kitchen had extra-small appliances because that was all there was room for. We removed a tiny closet and were able to put a full-size stainless-steel refrigerator in its place. We were also able to install a full-sized stove and a small dishwasher.

We discovered the two small windows near the stove during the demo. They'd been covered up for years, but exposing them added light and an unexpected original detail.

VINTAGE JARS FILLED WITH TREATS ARE GREAT FOR DESIGN AND SNACKING.

By tearing down the wall between the kitchen and the living room, we opened up both spaces.

EVERY KITCHEN NEEDS A ROOSTER.

THIS WAS A PIECE DAVID ALREADY OWNED; IT LOOKS GREAT AS A KITCHEN ISLAND.

PERFECT INDUSTRIAL PENDANTS ARE A GREAT POP OF COLOR.

CAESARSTONE COUNTERS ARE AS ATTRACTIVE AS AND MUCH CHEAPER THAN MOST HIGH-END COUNTERTOP MATERIALS.

ASK THE EXPERT
MARIO BATALI

We asked chef Mario Batali for his thoughts on creating the perfect kitchen.

Q: When it comes to kitchen appliances, does more expensive mean better?

A: Sometimes, but not always. I love my KitchenAid mixer, but a handheld mixer will do in many cases. It really depends on the intensity of the use—for example, if you're baking basic cakes and cookies, a handheld mixer is just fine. But if you're making bread or sausage, you need more torque, more force, which usually means a more expensive machine.

Q: Any thoughts on maximizing a small kitchen?

A: I love the idea of having wide, flat shelves to store baking sheets and flat pans along the floor molding—it's free space that is rarely used.

Q: Is it about the kitchen or the cook?

A: Only an amateur blames the equipment. A good cook can make anything almost anywhere. (Though a nice setup makes it easier—and easier to clean!)

Q: Why is the kitchen the most important room in the house?

A: The kitchen is where people spend most of their time—for meals, of course, but also almost every social gathering happens in the kitchen, whether it's a casual get-together or a Super Bowl shebang. The kitchen is a home's beating heart.

Q: Modern or vintage?

A: I like new stuff when I need to replace something, but it's hard to beat something with its own soul and history. One thing to remember: Good cooking is simply heat transfer, and good storage is all about refrigeration. Four burners, a cold fridge, some nice work space with a deep sink, and a kitchen is born.

ARRANGING THE BOOKS BY COLOR MAKES THEM STAND OUT AGAINST THE WHITE SHELVES.

STEP 2

DECORATE THE LIVING ROOM

David had some great furniture that we kept, but the couch was one of the pieces we replaced—it was just too big and bulky. The new sofa from CB2, with its clean lines, is a much better fit for the space.

We fell in love with an oversized chandelier from ABC Carpet and Home and knew it would make the perfect statement for this living room. Even with a small apartment, you can go big with your lighting. The chandelier looks as if it has always been there, and is the perfect feminine piece to balance the masculine details.

David's apartment is on the first floor of the building and level with the street, so for years he had a large pull-down shade and had to choose between privacy and natural light, which is a tough decision in the middle of Manhattan. We took down his existing shade and replaced it with a simple white top-down/bottom-up shade that makes a world of difference and can provide light and privacy.

BIG ART MAKES AN EVEN BIGGER STATEMENT WHEN IT'S THE FIRST THING YOU SEE IN A ROOM.

THE SOFA'S LOW PROFILE ALLOWS THE ART TO SHINE.

ORIGINAL DETAILS ARE WHAT MAKE AN OLD HOME FEEL SPECIAL.

DAVID IS A COLLECTOR, SO WE KEPT QUITE A FEW OF HIS BELONGINGS AND INCLUDED THEM THROUGHOUT THE SPACE.

RECONCEIVE THE BEDROOM

The bedroom was small, and David needed a work space. By hanging his bike on the wall and having California Closets build a custom floor-to-ceiling wardrobe, we were able to bring a desk into the bedroom. We had the desk custom made at City Foundry. With a reclaimed wood top that we were able to have cut to just the right size and an industrial metal base that was slightly higher than that of a typical desk, David's existing industrial-style bar stool was the perfect fit.

THIS LAMP IS FROM ABC CARPET AND HOME.

A ROTATING ART INSTALLATION

ONE-OF-A-KIND EMBROIDERED TOILE PILLOWS ADD COLOR AND HUMOR.

THE DESK WAS
CUSTOM MADE BY
CITY FOUNDRY
IN BROOKLYN.

YES,
THAT'S
AN
EMMY.

THE MEDICINE
CABINET IS
FROM OLDE
GOOD THINGS.

STEP 4

GUT THE BATHROOM

We got rid of the old sink and toilet and replaced all the existing tile with simple white subway tile. We took out the bathtub (which is a risk for resale, but since the apartment is a one-bedroom, we thought it was worth it) and replaced it with a large glass shower that takes up less space. We also avoided a big vanity sink and chose a pedestal sink that looks much more high-end because we replaced the hardware. The vintage medicine cabinet is perfectly industrial and looks sharp against the white tile.

TIPPER GORE

We asked Tipper Gore, who is a photographer, to give her tips on taking great photographs.

Photography is my passion. It's my chosen form of self-expression. It inspires, motivates, and moves me. I've been fortunate to have had opportunities to photograph for a newspaper, to freelance, and to document a wide variety of people, places, and wildlife throughout the years. Focusing my lens on nature has deepened my respect for the diversity and beauty that exists in our world. With every photo I take, I feel more profoundly connected to life itself.

Here are some ideas to consider:

- Open your eyes to the world around you. You'll find beauty everywhere: in flowers, trees, animals, sunrises, sunsets, rain, mist, clouds, pets, and people. Make prints of your favorite images to decorate your home.

- There are stories to be captured in less than ideal circumstances—after a fire or a flood, in a melting glacier or a dry riverbed. Your images can help others see the world in a different light, perhaps even moving them to join efforts to bring about change.

- Close-ups can capture interesting patterns and textures that are often missed. Tree bark, leaves, rocks, rippling water, and flower petals are part of nature's graphic designs.

- Document the passage of time by shooting the same scene in different seasons, or at different times of the year. Use the images to create an interesting series of prints.

- Experiment with sunlight at different times of day. Look at something from a higher or lower perspective than you normally would. Use your imagination to see the world in a new way.

- Wildlife photography requires preparation. Familiarize yourself with the terrain, with possible changes in weather and light, and bring the right equipment and clothing. Be respectful of the animals, their patterns of behavior and habits. Always ask for permission before venturing onto private land. Set the stage as much as possible, considering composition, light, animal behavior. And be prepared to spend several hours to get that "wow" shot.

I believe that each of us has an artist within. So get started! Grab your camera, go outside, and find the beauty out there that's waiting for you.

THE WOOD CANOPY PROVIDES BOTH PRIVACY AND ROMANCE.

AFTER: HAPPY

SIMPLE AND RUSTIC

DECORATE THE BACKYARD

David's backyard was gorgeous and a complete luxury in Manhattan, but he didn't have any place to sit, eat, or hang out with friends. There was a table that sat unused in the corner, but it was falling apart, and his plastic chairs were in bad shape. The budget for the backyard was fairly small, so we came up with a few creative solutions to transform it into a space he would enjoy and use.

We asked a friend of ours, artisan John Houshmand, to help with the woodwork. He brought an enormous slab of wood from upstate New York and attached it to the top of David's existing table, which he reinforced for better support. John also created the woven floating wood canopy above the table.

BEFORE: SAD

WE FOUND THIS WINDOW DURING DEMO. FINALLY— LIGHT!

WHITE CABINETS ARE CLEAN AND SIMPLE.

ANOTHER FUN WAY TO STORE WINE: IN A VINTAGE CRATE

WHERE WE ENDED

The place had great bones and a ton of charm. By knocking down the wall between the kitchen and the living room and bringing in art, lighting, and new furniture, we were able to give David an updated space that still honored the history of his home.

FLOWERS ADD COLOR.

IDEAS AND TIPS

IDEAS FOR REDOING A BATHROOM ON A BUDGET

- White subway tile is a sleek, clean, and inexpensive tile option. If you have a more flexible budget, do a focal wall or a strip in a more expensive tile.

- Inexpensive sinks, toilets, and tubs do pretty much the same thing as high-end versions and often look fairly similar.

- If you can't afford a really nice vanity, use a pedestal sink. Cheap vanities look cheap.

- Glass looks much better than a shower curtain.

- A single beautiful light goes a long way.

- Antique medicine cabinets and cool vintage mirrors look fantastic above the sink.

TIPS ON KITCHEN RENOVATIONS

- More expensive doesn't mean that much better. Stainless steel always looks great but does not need to be high-end.

- Simple and inexpensive cabinetry can look high-end, especially if you add tasteful hardware.

- Expensive countertops are overrated. Simple CaesarStone always looks gorgeous.

- A cool piece of vintage furniture can make a one-of-a-kind kitchen island.

- Bookshelves are useful for storing dishes and glassware or even as a pantry.

- Inexpensive vintage lighting adds character to contemporary kitchens.

- Your appliances do not all need to be the same brand. Use what looks good.

- Keep the floor plan open; everyone wants to be able to talk to their guests while cooking.

BUDGET ANALYSIS

	CONTRACTOR FEES	$70,762.05
	FLOORING AND CARPETS	$119.56
	WINDOW TREATMENTS	$1,740.91
	LIGHTING	$4,123.71
	CLOSET SYSTEM & WARDROBE	$4,726.05
	KITCHEN REMODEL	$13,135.69
	KITCHEN ACCESSORIES	$644.59
	BATHROOM REMODEL	$7,186.57
	FURNITURE	$6,482.73
	ART	$1,500.30
	HOME ACCESSORIES	$4,510.66
	BEDDING AND TOWELS	$1,115.32
	TOTAL	**$116,048.14**

NEW YORK
CITY GOES TO
OKLAHOMA

Pioneering Attic

Ree Drummond, also known as The Pioneer Woman, and her husband, Ladd, invited us to their ranch in rural Oklahoma to create a new bedroom for their two daughters, Alex, thirteen, and Paige, eleven. Ree and Ladd live on a large working cattle ranch with their four children and hundreds of animals, mostly cattle, but also horses (wild mustangs as well as domestic horses) and many cats and dogs. Their house—the same house that Ladd and his two brothers grew up in—was built in the early 1970s. It's a large, inviting, and incredibly warm place that stands on their breathtaking land, surrounded by the Oklahoma plains. We'd never worked in this part of the country before and were excited for the adventure.

WHERE WE STARTED

THE BUDGET
$25,000

THE GOAL
To transform a long, narrow storage room into a bedroom for two young girls

THE CLIENTS' WISH LIST

1. A space the girls could call their own

2. To replace the orange carpet

3. Closet storage space for clothing

4. An area for schoolwork and crafts

5. Girly feminine touches

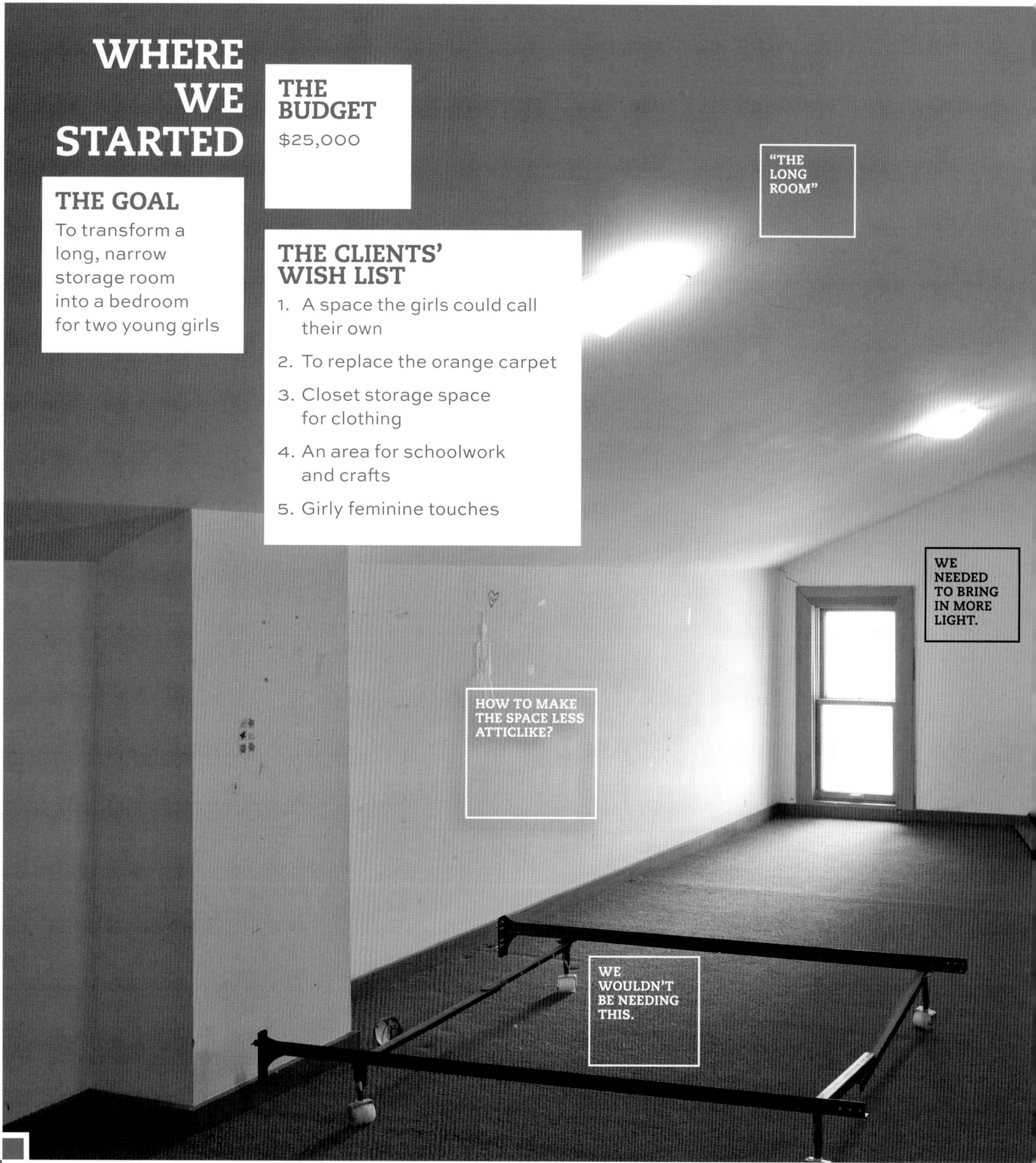

"THE LONG ROOM"

WE NEEDED TO BRING IN MORE LIGHT.

HOW TO MAKE THE SPACE LESS ATTICLIKE?

WE WOULDN'T BE NEEDING THIS.

We wanted to build the ultimate girls' bedroom.

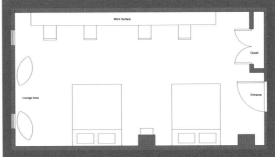

Before we began our work, the girls shared the upstairs—a large open space with three small, doorless, cubby-type bedrooms—with their two younger brothers, Todd, nine, and Bryce, seven. Needless to say, the girls were eager for a place of their own.

The plan was to move the girls into a separate, unoccupied room off of this space. It had always been used for storage, and because it's very narrow and extremely long, the family referred to it as "the long room." By the time we arrived, it had been emptied out; all that remained was the orange wall-to-wall carpeting, a reminder of the decade in which it was laid.

We wanted to build the ultimate girls' bedroom: a place where Alex and Paige could sleep, study, create, and hang out with friends. Our goal was to bring in the girls' personalities through color and fun furnishings and to keep a sense of openness. The shape of the room was a challenge—not only was it long and narrow, but the ceiling also sloped on one side. The upside was that the door and closet were at one end, while the two windows were on the opposite wall, which left a lot of space in between.

We loved working with the Drummonds because they gave us the green light to go wild with the room and take design risks. After spending some time with Ree, Ladd, and their kids, we realized that they were the country version of us—an active family living amid chaos but loving every minute of it.

DEMOLITION

Before we could begin, we had to strip down what was left. First we pulled out the orange wall-to-wall carpeting. And because the room had been mainly used for storage, the walls were in bad shape and needed to be repaired. After we fixed the walls, we painted them white. Then we were ready for action.

With not enough in our budget to lay a new floor, we replaced the carpet with blue "Ins and Outs" Flor carpet tiles. The bold blue kept the room from feeling too girly, and although there's a lot going on in this pattern, it's almost so busy it becomes neutral and grounds everything on top of it.

The existing closet was fairly deep but had only one hanging bar and no storage, shelving, or doors. It was just a lot of dead space and was perfectly suited for the custom shelving we installed. We finished it off with closet doors that were painted white to match the rest of the room.

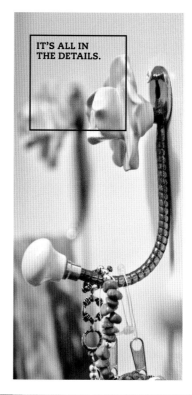

IT'S ALL IN THE DETAILS.

THE BLUE STRIPES ARE A PERFECT BACKDROP FOR THE REST OF THE ROOM.

WE FOUND SOME
GOOD LUCK FOR THE
GIRLS AT A NEARBY
ANTIQUES STORE.

THESE HIVE
SHELVES FROM
CB2 ARE
PERFECT FOR
THE GIRLS'
MANY PAIRS
OF COWBOY
BOOTS.

EVERY PARENT SHOULD STOP TIME AND GET A PAINTING DONE OF THEIR CHILD.

THE FOUR PAIRS OF PILLOWCASES FROM LAYLA ARE MADE FROM A COMBINATION OF VINTAGE TEXTILES AND HER OWN PRINTED PIECES.

STEP 2
INSTALL HANGING BEDS

Our goal was to maintain an airy feel, so we hired a local craftsman, Carl Engel, to build the hanging beds out of iron and wood to reflect the aesthetic of the Drummond ranch. Installing the beds was an enormous challenge—they were incredibly heavy and needed to be attached to the beams in the ceiling. The open space under the beds makes the room feel less crowded.

Instead of going crazy with pink and frilly girly bedding, we chose simple but beautiful fabrics in muted country colors. They show off the beds yet keep things feminine and sweet.

The green nesting tables between the beds are bold and functional, while the bunny lamp is playful and provides enough light to read by.

Our good friend Linda Mason, a New York–based artist, painted the portraits of the girls that hang above the beds. We thought this was a special way to introduce personal art.

THE THROWS ARE MADE BY BRAHMS MOUNT.

THE BEDSPREADS ARE EACH ONE-OF-A-KIND INDIAN HAND-LOOMED PIECES.

GREEN AND BLUE ARE GREAT TOGETHER.

Installing the beds was an enormous challenge.

ASK THE EXPERT
LINDA MASON

Artist Linda Mason has been a friend of ours since our early days in Manhattan. We asked her to talk about creating portraits of kids.

Q: Why do people love paintings of children so much?

A: When we love our child, there are moments that we would like to keep forever. Great portrait artists capture one of these beautiful moments and fix it on canvas so that everyone can look at the painting and, even if it is not their child, see the child's essence, character, and beauty. It's deeper than a photograph.

Q: What inspired you to start painting children?

A: I have always loved children, and I trained as a children's nurse many, many years ago. But I was first inspired to paint them by the love I felt for my daughter, Daisy.

Q: Is there a standard size your paintings come in?

A: The sizes of acrylic on canvas that I do most often are 18 inches by 24 inches, 18 inches by 18 inches, and 24 inches by 36 inches, depending on the child. I prefer these sizes because they may be larger than life if the child is young but not so big that the viewer is overwhelmed.

Q: Is it easier to paint from a photo or a live sitting?

A: I must admit that originally I would only paint from photographs that I took myself. This process would enable me "to get to know" the subject, so to speak. I do still prefer this, but I will work from photos clients have sent in. A variety of photos with some close-ups on the eyes are useful, especially because the photos are used more often as inspiration.

Q: Is there a perfect age for a portrait?

A: From ten months upward. At ten months, babies have a strong personality and are so relaxed. I find the early teens not impossible but the most difficult, as the children are going through a transition and aren't so relaxed and comfortable with themselves. But every age is interesting, so it's hard to say. I think that the parent is a good judge.

THE PURPLE CUBBIES HELP TO SUPPORT THE DESK AND ALSO PROVIDE COLORFUL STORAGE.

STEP 3

BUILD A LONG DESK

We asked Carl Engel to build a desk using the same local materials he used to build the beds, and he came back with the stunning sixteen-foot-long desk that runs most of the length of the room. The supports below were built as storage cubbies, and we painted them purple to bring in color and make the desk feel a little younger. We added the white shelf above to give the girls a place for their books, photos, collections, and awards.

Because Alex and Paige both like to sew and knit, we reserved one end of the long desk as a craft space. We created a yarn wall, added storage for needles and supplies, and made space for their sewing machine.

CARVE OUT A NOOK

Our goal for the area below the windows was to create a nook where the girls could hang out, read, knit, and spend time with their friends. We papered the wall behind it with a paint-by-numbers wallpaper designed by Jenny Wilkinson. It's gorgeous whether it's colored in or not, but we added a big basket of paint markers in case the girls felt inspired.

The beanbag chairs are Sitonit Originals made by Loopee Design. They're great for lounging and can be laid flat as extra beds for sleepovers.

The chandelier came from the River City Trading Post in Jenks, Oklahoma. Ree had always wanted a beautiful chandelier, but Ladd didn't think it would look right on a ranch, until this one found a home upstairs. It was the perfect way to define the nook as its own space.

PAINT-BY-NUMBERS WALLPAPER MAKES IT OKAY TO COLOR ON THE WALLS.

EVERY GIRL NEEDS A CHANDELIER.

A MAGAZINE RACK IS A GREAT WAY TO STORE AND DISPLAY FABRIC.

WHERE WE ENDED

The space was so long and narrow that we needed to think outside the box to create a room for Alex and Paige with enough space to sleep, work, and relax. We took the beds off the floor and went big with the desk. It's great to make a dramatic gesture, and all our risks paid off here.

A LIGHTER WALL COLOR COMPLETELY OPENS UP THE SPACE.

SISTERS' BEDDING SHOULD COORDINATE, NOT MATCH.

MIXING WOOD AND IRON FOR A GIRLY BEDROOM IS TOTALLY FAB.

WE LOVE THIS DINING CHAIR FROM PROPERTY, WHICH IS MADE COMPLETELY OUT OF RUBBER.

HOW TO

USE PAINT-BY-NUMBERS WALLPAPER

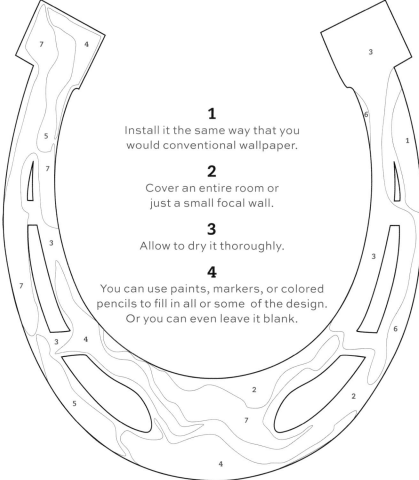

1

Install it the same way that you would conventional wallpaper.

2

Cover an entire room or just a small focal wall.

3

Allow to dry it thoroughly.

4

You can use paints, markers, or colored pencils to fill in all or some of the design. Or you can even leave it blank.

BUDGET ANALYSIS

CONTRACTOR FEES	$15,000.00
PAINT AND WALLPAPER	$240.00
FLOORING AND CARPETS	$1,918.40
WINDOW TREATMENTS	$470.00
LIGHTING	$655.40
FURNITURE	$3,554.90
MATTRESSES AND BEDDING	$1,064.00
ART	GIFT
HOME ACCESSORIES	$1,875.18
DESK ACCESSORIES	$383.00
CRAFT SUPPLIES AND STORAGE	$2,157.96
TOTAL	$27,318.84

HE LIKES MASCULINE INDUSTRIAL TOUCHES.

SHE PREFERS WARM AND COZY.

Hipster Haven

Pat Cook, a designer and brand manager for DQM (a skateboard/ skate-wear company), and his fiancée, Rika Shimada, a graphic designer, contacted us shortly after they purchased their first apartment, a two-bedroom, two-bathroom condo in a four-story walk-up in Williamsburg, Brooklyn. This was their first real home, and they were eager to move in but unsure of what to do next.

Pat and Rika had distinct ideas about what they wanted their home to look like and were relying on us to combine their visions without making the place feel schizophrenic. Rika was looking for cozy, feminine touches (she wanted a girly chandelier), while Pat's aesthetic was more traditionally masculine (he wanted a black leather sectional and things that were industrial looking).

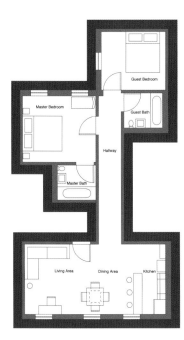

Luckily for us, these two were game for anything. They prepped us on their tastes, gave us their wish lists, and sent us off to go all out and do whatever we wanted.

Creating a home together is a wonderful step toward building a life as a couple. You learn a lot about the other person and what it means to be a team. Pat and Rika had moved in only a few weeks before we met them, and they were overwhelmed by the stuff that hadn't yet found a place in their new home. First we moved everything out of the main living area and master bedroom. Some things went to Goodwill, some to the second bedroom to be dealt with later, and the rest out on the curb.

Once the clutter was gone, the rooms seemed to be filled with possibilities. After more than twenty moves, we've learned that it is much easier to work in a cleared-out, empty space than to be surrounded and overrun by unpacked boxes and items that don't yet have a place to go.

These two needed just about everything—storage, lighting, furnishings, and art. For us, an unfurnished and undecorated apartment is a plus, a blank slate to go crazy on. Our biggest challenge would be the size of the space. The living area was only 400 square feet but would need to function as a living room, dining area, bar, and kitchen.

LOOKED
LIKE A
DORM ROOM

STILL TRYING
TO UNPACK
AND FIND
PLACES FOR
EVERYTHING

THIS KNOT PRINT—MADE BY RIKA—WAS A JUMPING-OFF POINT FOR OUR DESIGN.

WHERE WE STARTED

THE BUDGET

$15,000

THE GOAL

To transform an 870-square-foot white condo into an industrial-looking-yet-cozy home

THE CLIENTS' WISH LIST

1. Kitchen storage
2. Vintage lighting
3. New furniture
4. A combined aesthetic

Pat and Rika were overwhelmed by the stuff that hadn't yet found a place in their new home.

A VINTAGE CHANDELIER SOFTENS NEW CONSTRUCTION.

THE RED BAR CART ADDED COLOR AS WELL AS SURFACE AREA.

STEP 1
ADD KITCHEN STORAGE

The kitchen had a few wonderful pluses. It was open to the main living area, which made it feel bigger than it was, and the appliances and cabinetry were new and modern. The downside was that there was very little storage, so as soon as anything was purchased, from groceries to kitchen items, it looked cramped and messy.

We solved the storage problem by purchasing two freestanding vintage pieces that fit perfectly in the empty space near the stove. The white cabinet serves as a countertop for the cool pink microwave and also contains drawers and shelves for silverware, pots, and pans, while the stainless-steel barrister bookcase adds even more storage and is in keeping with the industrial feel Pat liked.

TRY TO SHOP LOCALLY—KEEP MOM-AND-POP SHOPS ALIVE.

USE VINTAGE PIECES FOR STORAGE THAT STANDS OUT.

We solved the storage problem by purchasing two vintage pieces.

THE PERFECT
MIX OF
INDUSTRIAL
AND COZY

IT'S OKAY
TO MIX AND
MATCH
DIFFERENT
DINING CHAIRS.

CREATE A DINING SPACE

We created a dining area near the windows using the existing table and two chairs. We added two more old-school wooden chairs that we purchased from Sunday Love, a nearby vintage store. Mixing the two sets of chairs took the focus away from the table, which was functional but not exciting.

Pat loves wine, so we hung an antique French wine rack above the counter and filled it with a few wine bottles and flowers for a playful touch.

THESE ARE FROM PIER 1 IMPORTS.

STEP 3

DECORATE THE LIVING ROOM

The challenge here was the size of the space, and our goal was to make it as hip as possible yet still sophisticated. We found a black leather sectional for Pat and added an array of pillows to soften it up. The mirrored end table and stool bring out the metallics in the pillows and the detailing on the bottom of the sofa. A black-and-white rug tied the whole thing together.

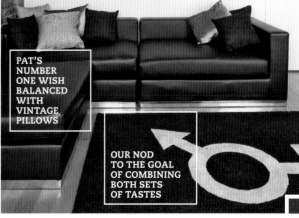

PAT'S NUMBER ONE WISH BALANCED WITH VINTAGE PILLOWS

OUR NOD TO THE GOAL OF COMBINING BOTH SETS OF TASTES

VINTAGE PRINT OF MICK JAGGER: $30.
GOLD-LEAF FRAME: $30.

THE WALLPAPER IS FROM MATTER, IN SOHO. HEXAGONS ARE ELEGANT AND HIP.

STEP 4

DECORATE THE BEDROOM

The bedroom looked like it belonged to a couple of college kids. It was empty aside from a bed, a rug, a few suitcases, and a pile of junk on the floor. The bed had no frame and was held up by cement blocks, the walls were bare, and a single lightbulb hung from the ceiling. We bought an inexpensive bed frame and new bedding to complement the sophisticated dark color palette we were using. We replaced the bulb with a beautiful antique pendant, and went to work on the rest of the furniture, the walls, and the ceiling. Our goal was to transform the space into something that resembled a hip Parisian hotel room.

Because we were on a budget, we decided to wallpaper only behind the bed, thereby making that wall the room's focal point. Papering one wall also allows you to go bolder than if you were to do an entire room.

A LITTLE GAUDY IS A GOOD THING.

WE SAVED MONEY BY REUPHOLSTERING A TATTERED CHAISE USING FABRIC REMNANTS.

THIS DRAWING ON BLACK CHALKBOARD PAINT IS BY JAMES SEWARD.

Our goal was to transform the space into something that resembled a hip Parisian hotel room.

LET ME

WH

YOUR

THE COLLECTION
OF VINTAGE
MIRRORS MAKES
THE SPACE FEEL
MUCH LARGER.

THE COLLECTION
OF VINTAGE
MIRRORS MAKES
THE SPACE FEEL
MUCH LARGER.

DECORATE WITH
YOUR HOME'S
ORIGINAL DETAILS
IN MIND.

WHERE WE ENDED

Many couples are in search of a look that marries their sensibilities. Combining vintage and modern, such as the chandeliers and a collection of flea-market mirrors on the brick wall with the black sectional, is a great way to go about finding that middle ground.

THIS PHRASE
WAS AN INSIDE
JOKE BETWEEN
PAT AND RIKA—
NOW THEIR
PERSONALITIES
HAVE BECOME
PART OF
THE DESIGN.

DON'T BE
AFRAID TO
CARRY
THE PAINT
ONTO
THE DOOR.

SPER IN

. . . EAR?

JAMES SEWARD

We asked artist James Seward how to create chalkboard art.

Q: How do you draw on chalkboard paint?

A: There are several options. You can either draw the image freehand, which takes great artistic skill, or you can transfer a drawing. Transferring saves time, it's more accurate, and it's a great option for those who find drawing a challenge. This is how you do it:

1. Choose the drawing that you are going to transfer. If it's not the desired size, get a large photocopy made.
2. Cover the back of the drawing with chalk.
3. Tape the drawing in place so that the paper remains stable.
4. Run a stylus or anything hard but blunt (like a teaspoon handle) along the lines of the drawing on the front to transfer it.

Remember to be patient with yourself, have fun, and let your imagination run wild.

Q: Does it require sealing or a special coat of polyurethane?

A: I personally do not seal my chalk drawings because it slightly dulls the value of the pigment. But if you do decide to use a fixative, make sure you apply it in smooth, even coats. Crystal Clear and Krylon spray fixatives are two good options. If you're going to use one, make sure you have plenty of ventilation— the fumes can make your head feel fuzzy inside.

Q: Do the drawings erase easily, like chalk on a chalkboard?

A: Yes, they do. You may have to use a little elbow grease on older drawings—there is subtle bonding that occurs with the chalk and the chalkboard paint if you leave the chalk up for a while.

Q: What type of chalk do you use?

A: Regular chalk does a fine job, but if you want brighter hues, I suggest hard pastels. They come in a variety of colors, and their pigment strength far exceeds that of regular chalk. But they are a bit pricey. Rembrandt is a great brand, though there are a variety of brands that range in quality and price.

HOW TO

HANG A WINE RACK
(OR ANY HEAVY PIECE)

When hanging anything that weighs as much as a wine rack (especially a full wine rack), take precautions—like reinforcing the wall behind it so that the piece doesn't pull out of the wall. If the wall is framed in wood, the framing will support the heavy object. If the wall is framed in metal, then heavy objects need to be attached to something stronger than the framing. Most new construction is framed in metal because of fire codes.

ADD SUPPORTS
Cut a hole in the Sheetrock and attach a two-by-four (or other heavy piece of wood) to the frame (if it's wood framing) or to the inside of the exterior wall (if it's metal framing). The extra wood will support the weight and keep the wall in place.

MODIFY THE RACK
For wine racks, attach a piece of wood to the back of the rack somewhere near the top. The wood will allow the rack to hang at an angle so that the bottles will fit once it's on the wall.

WHEN IN DOUBT . . .
If you are unsure about a wall's capacity to handle the weight, ask an expert to install the rack for you. Something as heavy as a full wine rack hung incorrectly can be dangerous to the walls and to anyone standing nearby.

BUDGET ANALYSIS

CONTRACTOR FEES	$5,965.30
PAINT AND SUPPLIES	$185.05
WALLPAPER	$319.00
RUG	GIFT
LIGHTING	$928.31
FURNITURE	$5,902.54
BEDDING	$217.72
ARTIST FEE	$200.00
ART	$1,405.39
ACCESSORIES	$184.95
TOTAL	**$15,308.26**

RUBY

SUZANNE

Reader's Refuge

Singer-songwriter Suzanne Vega has been a close friend of ours since the mid-1990s, when she rented a town house that we'd renovated in the Chelsea neighborhood of Manhattan. It was the first project we'd ever done and marked the beginning of our careers as builders and designers. Once we'd finished it, we moved into the garden-floor apartment, and Suzanne and her daughter, Ruby, lived upstairs (yes, on the second floor). That was many years ago, long before she moved to her current home, which is a gorgeous prewar co-op on the Upper West Side of Manhattan.

The apartment has beautiful bones, tons of intricate detailing, and an open floor plan through the common spaces. Suzanne asked us to help her redesign and organize the living room and the music

BARE WALLS

HOMELESS BOOKS

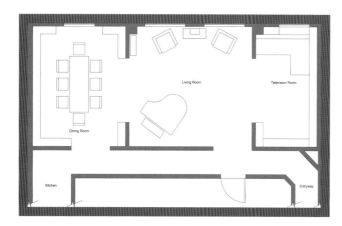

room/library. The main issue was decluttering. Suzanne's home was filled with oversized furniture, books, instruments, photos, and relics that she had acquired over the years.

Our first task was to clear it all out. We donated most of the furniture, and many of the smaller decorative and personal items went to storage. We kept only the best and most meaningful items and made it our mission to put them on display so they could be enjoyed and appreciated.

WHERE WE STARTED

THE BUDGET
$12,000

THE GOAL
To organize and open up the space, making it chic, bright, and more functional

THE CLIENT'S WISH LIST

1. To reintroduce fun through the two rooms

2. To organize the books and library

3. To showcase family photos and awards

4. To find the piano!

5. To give the space a design upgrade

MORE BOOKS

OVERSIZED FURNITURE LEAVES VERY LITTLE OPEN FLOOR SPACE.

THE BOOKS LOOKED GREAT ONCE THEY WERE ORGANIZED.

A FEW WELL-CHOSEN ACCESSORIES ADD INTEREST TO THE SHELVES.

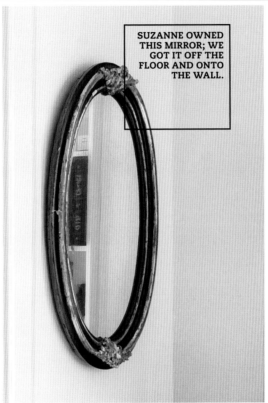

SUZANNE OWNED THIS MIRROR; WE GOT IT OFF THE FLOOR AND ONTO THE WALL.

STEP 1
REORGANIZE THE LIBRARY

Suzanne has hundreds of books. They were overflowing from the shelves, piled on coffee and side tables, and stacked on every other flat surface in between. She calls her books her friends, so we knew that we had to treat them gently and find homes for all of them. First we removed all the books and decorative items from the shelves. We sorted through and matched the books by size and genre, then put them back. When we ran out of space, neat piles of books were stacked on top of the shelves.

We had our carpenter build
a custom L-shaped sofa.

WE PAINTED
THE DAYBED
"GYPSY PINK"—
A GREAT SPLASH
OF COLOR.

THE CUSHIONS ARE FUN
AND TIE IN TO THE PAINT.

WE ADDED BACK
BOOK STORAGE
WHERE THE
CUSTOM SOFA
BLOCKED SHELVES.

STEP 2

DESIGN AND BUILD
CUSTOM FURNITURE

Our sofa options for the library were limited to whatever would fit the narrow space. Not wanting to sacrifice style for a piece that would work simply because it was the right size, we had our carpenter, Tom Baione, build a custom L-shaped sofa. The cushions were made out of a gold-flocked diamond fabric from Mood Designer Fabrics in New York.

STEP 3
PROPERLY DISPLAY THE INSTRUMENTS

We moved the piano from the library to the living room, which both opened up the library and showcased the piano. It had taken up almost the entire library, leaving no room to hang out and read. Moving the piano out into the larger space also made it the focal point of the room—which makes sense when it's Suzanne Vega's home.

HOW SWEET THE SOUND

BIG FURNITURE (OR INSTRUMENTS) SHOULD BE PLACED IN BIG SPACES.

ASK THE EXPERT
SUZANNE VEGA

We asked Suzanne Vega to talk about the importance of music.

Q: You come from an ultra-creative family—how did that influence you?

A: My stepfather was a novelist and short story writer and he wrote a few songs and played the guitar, which I always liked. My mother is a computer systems analyst. They both encouraged us to be as creative and as educated as possible. My birth father also has a strong musical talent.

Q: Why should we have music in our homes?

A: There are some people, believe it or not, who don't like music! But I love music, and it can make you feel connected to humanity without the use of words.

Q: Is having music playing on your stereo as important as having art on your walls?

A: It's more personal in some ways—you can have art to impress someone else, but usually you listen to music for yourself.

Q: Your piano is a focal point in your home. Does it have a story?

A: Our piano is very special because it comes from my husband Paul's family and it is a Steinway from a hundred years ago. It was a gift to us from his parents when we got married in 2006.

STEP 4
LIGHT THE LIVING ROOM

The existing brass chandelier didn't work and was (literally) falling out of the ceiling. It was a beautiful piece and Suzanne liked it, so instead of replacing it, we had it rewired and powder-coated green. It looks modern while still retaining its elegance and makes the space feel less serious.

POWDER-COATING CAN TRANSFORM PIECES YOU ALREADY HAVE.

ASK THE EXPERT
LAWRENCE CARTER

We asked Lawrence Carter, the owner of Carter Spray Finishing Corp., a few questions about powder-coating.

Q: What prep work is necessary before powder-coating?

A: All prior paint finishes must be removed to assure a quality powder-coat finish. The usual method is sandblasting.

Q: What materials can be powder-coated?

A: Only metallic substrates such as steel, aluminum, or bronze can be powder-coated. And all parts must be able to be hung by a hook for electrostatic purposes.

Q: Is it possible to powder-coat something in a custom color?

A: Yes. Custom powders can be made to match almost all colors in gloss to flat. The minimum charge for a color match is seven hundred dollars.

Q: Why is powder-coating better than spray-painting a piece of furniture?

A: Powder-coating is a cross-linked thermosetting polymer (think epoxy or polyurethane), which is twice as thick and many times stronger than paint.

Q: What's the craziest thing you've ever powder-coated?

A: A 10-foot hot tub—4 feet deep.

Q: How long does the whole powder-coating process take?

A: Not long. Ten lamp bases, for example, in flat black take a total of one hour from spraying to packing.

BEFORE

THE NEW WINDOW TREATMENTS DO A GOOD JOB OF HIDING THE AIR CONDITIONER.

THE VINTAGE CHAIRS WERE RESTUFFED AND REUPHOLSTERED.

CELEBRATE YOUR SUCCESS—DISPLAY ACHIEVEMENTS AND AWARDS WITH FAMILY PHOTOS.

STEP 5

DECORATE THE WALLS

The walls in both rooms were painted dull shades of yellow. We repainted them a crisp pale blue, which completely brightened up the space and highlighted the gorgeous crown molding. We hung one strip of wallpaper between the windows, which offsets the high-gloss black of the altar.

The existing drapes in the living room looked messy, so we replaced all the window treatments with simple, relaxed white linen roman shades. They are clean and elegant and showcase the beautiful prewar window frames.

WHERE WE ENDED

Clearing the clutter was most of the battle here, and once it was gone, the space was transformed entirely. So much of the floor space was regained that Suzanne's instruments, art, books, and family photos finally had the opportunity to stand out.

THE GREEN CHANDELIER LOOKS GREAT AGAINST THE WALL COLOR.

PIPING IS A CHANCE TO GO BOLD, LIKE WITH THIS CONTRASTING COLOR.

THESE PHOTOS WERE TAKEN BY PHOTOGRAPHER (AND SUZANNE'S BROTHER) MATTHEW VEGA.

ASK THE EXPERT

MATTHEW J. VEGA

We asked photographer Matthew J. Vega to give us some pointers on getting the shot.

- Know your camera and lens: Understanding their strong points and their limitations will help you make important decisions quickly. The best way to learn what the camera and lens do well is to take a lot of photographs in a variety of conditions.

- Light: Photography is all about light and how it describes the world visually. Examine the strength, color, and direction of the light, but, most important, notice how the light describes your subject.

- Timing: When photographing, be ready for anything. Study your surroundings and anticipate what is about to happen. Take a broad view and notice how things move in relation to one another. Have your camera ready!

- Subject: Treat your subject with the utmost respect and try to find that one view that transcends the ordinary. Every photograph you take is an opportunity to create an iconic image.

- Luck: There is an element of faith involved in photography. It is not always possible to predict the exact outcome of one's photographic efforts. Getting lucky now and again always helps.

Photograph by Matthew Vega

RULES FOR

DECLUTTERING

- Does it bring beauty to the space? If not, get rid of it.

- Does it hold special meaning for you? If not, get rid of it.

- Can you actually use it (e.g., VHS tapes)? If not, get rid of it.

- Spring-clean every season. Every three or four months, do a massive home purging.

- If you have attachment disorder with your stuff, have a friend or even a professional help you decide what needs to go.

- You can sell almost anything on Craigslist (just don't be greedy when setting the price).

- If you just can't part with something but it doesn't work in your space, put it into storage.

BUDGET ANALYSIS

CONTRACTOR FEES	$3,200.00
PAINT AND WALLPAPER	$302.05
WINDOW TREATMENTS	$606.00
LIGHTING	$780.00
FURNITURE	$5,170.00
FABRIC AND REUPHOLSTERY	$3,354.00
PIANO TUNING	$105.00
ART	$1,632.00
ACCESSORIES	$860.93
FLOWERS	$90.31
TOTAL	**$16,100.29**

MAJOR

BREAKER

FIVE

HOLLEDER

Tree House

Way back when we had only four children, we purchased a vacation home in Trancoso, Brazil. Since then, we've spent numerous vacations there. Aside from being our family's favorite place to escape to, the house is also an investment property; we rent it out most of the year, which pays for the mortgage and its upkeep.

Both our family and the town of Trancoso have grown quite a bit since we bought the house. There are many more people vacationing there, and more luxury homes are being built every year, most of which are available to rent. We visit at least twice a year, as it's the one place where we feel we can really relax and forget about the chaos of our lives in Manhattan.

WHERE WE STARTED

THE BUDGET
$35,000

THE GOAL
To create a small but multifunctional tree house in our front yard

OUR WISH LIST
1. A private bed and bath
2. Ocean views
3. To use local and sustainable woods
4. A tree house reminiscent of the one in *The Swiss Family Robinson*

THE TREE WAS NOT AS LARGE AS WE WOULD HAVE HOPED.

WE CHOSE A SPACE NEAR THE ENTRANCE OF THE MAIN HOUSE.

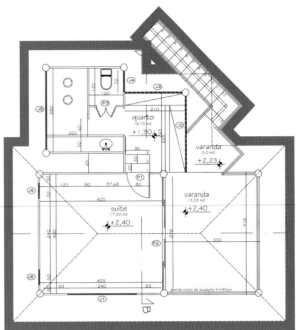

Our latest (and largest) project was the result of a suggestion by our eleven-year-old son, Breaker. He had recently seen *The Swiss Family Robinson,* and, like a lot of kids after seeing the film, he became obsessed with the idea of living in a tree house. And like most sane parents, we ignored him. But a few weeks later, we were having dinner at Uxua, a hotel in town, and found, to Breaker's delight, that one of the villas was an incredible, upscale tree house. As soon as we saw it, we understood his passion.

We called the same builders who had built the hotel and asked if they could do something similar for us. We justified the idea and the cost because we figured the tree house would increase the value of our property. Because Trancoso had become a popular vacation spot, our home was in competition with many other properties as a rental.

We chose the area near the entrance of the property to build on because it is somewhat secluded and has a nice tree.

Our main challenge, aside from finding a large-enough tree, was working out the scale of the house. We planned to fit a bedroom, a bathroom, a closet, and a large veranda in a 400-square-foot space surrounding a tree, overlooking the ocean from all sides. Once the location and the tree were chosen, construction began. Brazil has some of the most beautiful natural woods in the world, and most of them are incredibly expensive to import and build with anywhere else—so it was a luxury to be able to incorporate them into every aspect of the tree house.

BUILD THE BEDROOM

The bed was crafted using local woods so that it would blend into the rest of the structure. Thin wood rods with wires were installed on top of the bed in order to hang mosquito netting. Mosquito nets are a necessity in climates like Trancoso's—unless you want to live with all the windows and doors closed all the time. We actually love the look of mosquito netting, and the kids love sleeping in the "little tents." The bed linens are a muted yellow; it's a subtle color that doesn't overwhelm the space. And, because it's hot in Trancoso, pale colors and thin linens make the space feel cooler. The bedside tables were crafted locally, and the lamps on top were made from small tree trunks. The long, narrow shelf built into the wall near the bed is a rudder from an old boat. We also built the wood frame for the TV so that nothing looked too new, awkward, or out of place.

THIS BRAZILIAN FLAG BY ARTIST ANN CARRINGTON PROVIDES A GREAT POP OF COLOR FOR THE ROOM.

THANKS TO THE TALENTED LOCAL CRAFTSMEN, THE CEILING IS A WORK OF ART.

THE LINENS WERE PURCHASED LOCALLY—THEY BRING COLOR TO THE SPACE.

A FUN WAY TO HANG A FLAT-SCREEN

ASK THE EXPERT
ANDRE LATTARI

Contractor Andre Lattari and his crew of craftsmen, carpenters, and artisans built the tree house. We drew up the plans while we visited over spring break, and they finished in time for our arrival that August. We asked Andre to say a few words about the woods that he used and the process of creating the house itself.

"The structure itself was built with eucalyptus, which came from a reforestation project in the south of Bahia. The walls and windows are made with tatajuba, which is from the north of Brazil, and the roof is made from paraju, also from the north. We obtained permission and received a certificate from the government's environmental institute in order to build with local, sustainable woods.

"It was a pleasure building the tree house, a mix of fun and hard, detailed work, as the construction methods required an artisanal touch that brings out the rustic and charming aspects of the house. Fortunately, we had a fantastic team of highly skilled carpenters, real artists. It took us five months to get the house ready, from the initial architectural sketches to the Champagne on the veranda when it was complete."

BUILD THE BATHROOM

The bathroom is the only area in the tree house that doesn't have a view of the ocean, so we felt that it needed to be extra special.

The shower area is made of river stones. The showerhead is made of eucalyptus, as are the bathroom walls. The builders made the faucet out of a spare piece of copper pipe. There is a natural mix of beige-brown tones throughout the wood because it was treated with cement, which reinforces the artisanal approach.

We wanted to keep everything as simple as possible, with very little clutter. The bathroom sink is just a white basin attached to the top of an inexpensive farm table (we cut a hole in the table and ran the plumbing through). The shades for the lights above the toilet and sink and in the closet area were made locally out of straw baskets. We added only the necessities: the baskets underneath the sink for towels, and the simple wood-framed mirror above.

THE LIGHT FIXTURE WAS MADE FROM A WICKER BASKET.

A RUSTIC TABLE WAS TRANSFORMED INTO A SINK.

SIMPLE AND SLEEK

EUCALYPTUS SHOWERHEADS

LOCAL STONES WERE CEMENTED INTO THE SHOWER.

ASK THE EXPERT
BREAKER NOVOGRATZ

We asked our son Breaker for his thoughts on tree houses.

Q: What's the coolest tree house you've ever seen?
A: The tree house in *The Swiss Family Robinson*.

Q: Why do kids love tree houses?
A: Because they are little houses and they are away from your parents.

Q: What do you do in a tree house?
A: Watch movies all night, eat good food, and sleep in.

Q: If you were the builder, what would you have done differently to your tree house?
A: I would have built a zip line to the pool.

Q: What's your favorite thing about Brazil?
A: Cheese sticks on the beach.

Q: House or tree house?
A: Tree house. It's cooler.

There is a natural mix of beige-brown tones throughout the wood.

BUILD THE VERANDA

In tropical climates, outdoor space is as important as—if not more important than—indoor space, so we wanted the living and seating areas to all be outside but enclosed enough to be protected from the rain. The views from the porch are spectacular, so it only made sense to keep the space as open as possible. We made it simple yet cozy, so that it would be a great place to hang out and drink wine with friends at night as well as a place to play board games with the kids on a rainy day.

The white sofa is plain and a little bit boxy, so we dressed it up with a few bright pillows and blankets. The coffee table, lamp, and baskets were made locally. The refrigerator was a plain white minifridge until we framed it in wood so it would blend in with the surroundings.

WE USE THIS ROOM RAIN OR SHINE.

THE MINIFRIDGE KEEPS THE KIDS FROM RUNNING BACK AND FORTH TO THE MAIN HOUSE FOR DRINKS.

SWISS FAMILY ROBINSON, CIRCA 2012

The views from the porch are spectacular.

A COZY ESCAPE BENEATH THE TREE

STEP 4

BUILD THE HANGOUT BELOW

The tree house is fairly high off the ground, so we created a cozy little seating area below. It's a fun place for the kids to hang out, and we like it, too. We kept it as simple as possible, adding only a porch swing that hangs from above, two straw chairs with white cushions, and a coffee table. It's a great place to hide out and read a book when you've had too much sun and need an escape from your seven children.

WHERE WE ENDED

We built the space using natural Brazilian woods and did our best to avoid bringing in anything that can't be found in the local jungle (aside from a few luxuries like plumbing and TV). You can't compete with nature.

RENTALS HAVE QUADRUPLED SINCE WE BUILT THE TREE HOUSE.

AN OPEN FLOOR PLAN WORKS EVEN IN A TREE HOUSE.

THIS IS WHAT
YOU CALL
BRINGING THE
OUTSIDE IN.

TIPS AND TRICKS

TIPS FOR TREE HOUSES, POOL HOUSES, AND GUESTHOUSES

KEEP IT SIMPLE.
If it's not your primary house, don't stress over the little things.

LESS IS MORE.
There is no need for any clutter whatsoever in a guesthouse or tree house.

LET THE HOUSE BE THE ART PIECE.
Just add a few pops of color to brighten it up.

NEVER PUT A TON OF MONEY INTO FUN HOUSES.
They are meant to be fun, and not too precious or fragile.

DON'T SAVE THEM FOR GUESTS.
They're there for your use, too!

BUDGET ANALYSIS

CONTRACTOR FEES	$21,632.00
FLOORING AND CARPETS	$778.00
WINDOW TREATMENTS	$190.00
LIGHTING	$1,170.00
IRON PLATE FOR ROOF	$103.00
COPPER FIXTURES	$665.00
FURNITURE	$7,933.00
MATTRESS AND LINENS	$1,952.00
HAMMOCK	$130.00
ACCESSORIES	$383.00
MOSQUITO NETTING	$90.00
TOTAL	$35,026.00

HIGH CEILINGS
AND WHITE
WALLS COMMAND
BIG ART.

City
Reserve

Shane Konrad and Ryan McCormack are both doctors at Bellevue Hospital in New York City. We met them shortly after they'd moved into a brand-new, three-story town house in Williamsburg, Brooklyn. The place was modern with clean lines, big windows, and great light. But because both Shane and Ryan have incredibly hectic schedules—Shane is a forensic psychiatrist and Ryan is an emergency medicine physician—neither of them had any time to decorate, think about design, or shop for decor.

After they moved in, they furnished the apartment with a lot of post-college chairs and couches, items from past homes, quick-fix pieces, and artifacts from their travels. In their new home, nothing matched, and most of the furniture was either too big for the space or looked out of place in the clean modern interior.

WHERE WE STARTED

THE BUDGET
$35,000

THE GOAL
To create a modern space that is open and clean with a few pops of color

THE CLIENTS' WISH LIST

1. Much-needed storage for the kitchen
2. A deep, comfortable sofa
3. Color through accents and furnishings
4. A statement-making light fixture
5. An art collection

THIS ART WAS TOO SMALL—IT GOT LOST ON THE BIG WALL.

THE COUCH WAS TOO BULKY.

THE TABLE WAS DATED.

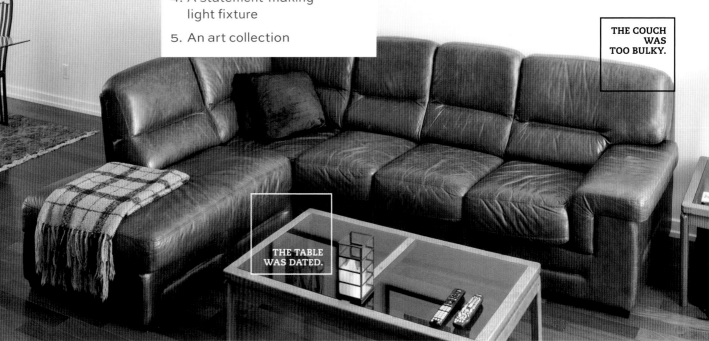

Most of the furniture was too big for the space.

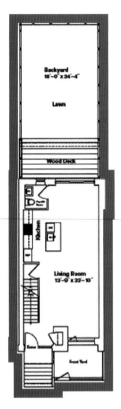

Shane and Ryan asked us to transform the main level of their house into a space where the interior furnishings would reflect the style of their home. They were both somewhat hesitant about color and wanted it used in a way that wouldn't overwhelm the home. They love nature and hoped that we could incorporate natural elements into the design.

THE SPACE
WAS BEGGING
TO GET
NOVOGRATZED.

THE BOOKS ADD A POP OF COLOR TO THE SPACE.

WITH NEW UPHOLSTERY, THESE CLUB CHAIRS ARE ONE OF A KIND.

THIS WAS DESIGNED BY CHRISTOPHER LABROOY.

THIS VINTAGE RUG WAS OVERDYED TO GIVE IT NEW LIFE.

STEP 1

DESIGN THE LIVING AREA

The existing living area had been taken over by a brown leather sectional that looked like a huge catcher's mitt. There was an unexciting coffee table paired with an unexciting side table. The furniture had to be replaced.

The navy sofa is from CB2, and we brightened it up with an assortment of colorful custom pillows in different shades of blue. The Milo Baughman club chairs were reupholstered, making them one of a kind, and the clear Plexiglas coffee table defines the seating area while showcasing the overdyed vintage rug from Still + Company.

The light above the kitchen counter was too big for the area. We replaced it with a small white ceramic pendant so that it wouldn't compete with the dining-room fixture.

WE FOUND THE
BLACK WIRE
LAMPS AT A
VINTAGE STORE
IN OKLAHOMA.

MICHAEL STROUT

We asked artisan Michael Strout to explain the what, where, and why of rug dyeing.

Q: Where do you find the rugs that you dye?

A: I source them from formal antique shows or auction galleries, and I find little gems among stoop sales in Brooklyn or yard sales throughout New England.

Q: Are there certain things that you look for when you are choosing a rug to dye?

A: None of the rugs are new, so we're always making sure they're in good shape, that the fibers aren't too worn and the weave is strong.

Q: Did it take a lot of experimenting to perfect the method?

A: Some of our first pieces came out surprisingly well. Over time, though, we knew we could refine the process to get stronger dye retention and higher color density and concentration. It was also about developing our willingness to take a risk and try something completely new. We have done a lot of dyeing and a lot of experimenting, but at the end of the day, each rug is going to act and dye differently, and we *want* each rug to be very much its own, without any "perfection."

PICK THE ART

Shane and Ryan had hung some art as placeholders, but the pieces didn't work in the space and were too small. Using art as a temporary quick fix can work against you, because it's easy to get used to it and then never replace it.

The two new large pieces of art came from Room 125 in Manhattan. All of their prints are made from the photographer's personal collection of antiques and artifacts, which are photographed and blown up to dramatic sizes.

The badminton birdie photograph is called *19th Century Shuttlecock,* and framed in reclaimed wood it makes an even bigger impact. The piece in the dining area, *Victorian Garnet Brooch,* is feminine and elegant over the industrial dining table.

UNIQUE LIGHTING IS A NOVOGRATZ SIGNATURE.

ASK THE EXPERT
SARAH HASTED
We asked Sarah Hasted, from the gallery Hasted Kraeutler, for her advice on hanging, framing, and lighting artwork.

Q: How high should art be hung?
A: The rule of thumb is to hang art 59 inches off the floor. I believe when you hang artwork in a home, the work should be hung at a height that feels comfortable in the room. People tend to hang artwork too high. You should never look up at artwork.

Q: What is your preferred method of framing?
A: We don't have one specific preference for framing. The frame should not overwhelm the artwork. I believe the frame should disappear but look sophisticated. That being said, I have no problem with putting a photograph in an ornate gold-leaf frame to make a statement. You do get what you pay for with frames. If you cheap out, it shows.

Q: What are your thoughts on large works of art?
A: I represent a number of artists who make very large works. I think if you have the wall space, you should be dramatic and hang a large piece of artwork, or five—it will look fantastic! Large works add a bit of drama to any room and are always a conversation starter.

USING
DIFFERENT
END CHAIRS
IS A GREAT
WAY TO MIX
THINGS UP.

NOW
THEY CAN
ENTERTAIN
IN STYLE.

STEP 3

DESIGN THE DINING AREA

The dining area had a glass table that was surrounded by six black metal chairs. It looked like a set from the 1980s and did not fit the space, nor did it fit with Shane and Ryan's aesthetic. They needed a dining space in which they could entertain friends and host dinner parties in style. Because they had the space, we gave them a larger table with a planked wood top and industrial legs. The six chairs on the sides of the wooden table were inexpensive (from CB2), and the two at the heads of the table are higher-end, from O & G Studios. And because Shane and Ryan love nature, we purchased a terrarium for the centerpiece.

The red locker behind the table came from Re*Pop in Brooklyn. It gives the space character and is an unexpected storage solution. The framed art on top of the locker is a collection of Boy Scout patches that we purchased on eBay and had framed. We are always looking for collections or random objects to frame. We love pieces with history.

SMALL POPS OF COLOR MAKE A BIG DIFFERENCE.

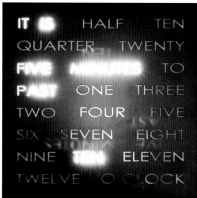

IT IS HALF TEN
QUARTER TWENTY
FIVE MINUTES TO
PAST ONE THREE
TWO FOUR FIVE
SIX SEVEN EIGHT
NINE TEN ELEVEN
TWELVE O'CLOCK

STEP 4

SPICE UP
THE KITCHEN

The kitchen was brand-new and just needed a few design elements to help bring it to life. The green mugs, the ink jug full of coffee beans, and the green and stainless coffeemaker are all small but effective ways to add color to the countertop.

The kitchen needed a few design elements to help bring it to life.

THESE GREAT
BRIGHT-BLUE
BAR STOOLS
ARE FUN AND
INVITING.

WHERE WE ENDED

Shane and Ryan's decor finally matched the modern setting of their home. By giving the walls a fresh coat of white paint, we created the perfect setting to showcase great statement pieces of furniture and incredible new art.

THIS IS MADE OF FELT AND ACRYLIC.

THE TABLE WILL LAST FOREVER.

GREAT LIGHT

NOTHING COMPARES WITH HAVING A REAL TREE INDOORS.

TIPS AND TRICKS

GREAT COLLECTIBLES TO FRAME

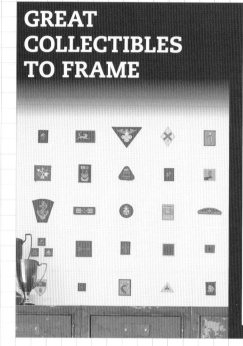

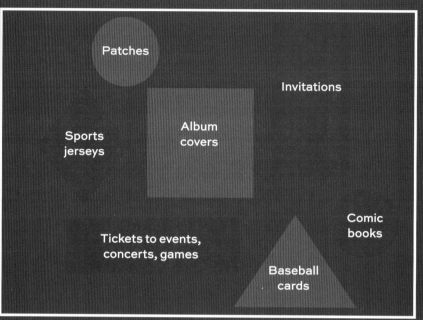

Patches

Invitations

Sports jerseys

Album covers

Comic books

Tickets to events, concerts, games

Baseball cards

BUDGET ANALYSIS

	CONTRACTOR FEES	$2,534.28
	PAINT	$87.07
	OVERDYED RUG	$1,360.94
	WINDOW TREATMENTS	$3,810.00
	LIGHTING	$1,668.09
	FURNITURE	$8,936.57
	VINTAGE LOCKER	$1,088.75
	FABRIC AND UPHOLSTERY	$2,832.12
	ART	$4,886.96
	ACCESSORIES	$1,879.58
	BOOKS	$1,254.53
	MISCELLANEOUS	$249.83
	TOTAL	**$30,588.72**

WOOF

Surf Shack

Deborah and Katherine Chen are sisters who live and work in Manhattan but have a second home in Far Rockaway, Queens. Far Rockaway has a small, tight-knit surfing community, and the girls, who both surf, fell in love with it. Their Queens home is an escape from their hectic, busy lives in the city, and they hope to move there full-time one day.

We met them shortly after they'd closed on this two-story, three-bedroom house. It had been in default and was in rough shape, so the Chens got a great deal. The house needed major renovations and a lot of interior work. The stairs were falling apart, floorboards were missing, the kitchen cabinets were broken and falling off the hinges, and there were no appliances whatsoever.

WHERE WE STARTED

THE BUDGET
$40,000

THE GOAL
To transform an old, broken-down house into a colorful, girly surfer cottage

THE CLIENTS' WISH LIST

1. A new staircase
2. A whole new kitchen
3. Window treatments for privacy
4. Decorative lighting
5. Tons of color, especially pink!

THE WALLS WERE PAINTED WITH DRAB BROWNS AND YELLOWS.

SOS (SAVE OUR STAIRS!)

Deborah and Katherine wanted us to create a girly, bohemian beach vibe; they complained that the house felt outdated and old. They're both young, adventurous, and up for anything, which made the project fun. Our goal was to create something youthful and larger than life to echo the girls' huge personalities. Our biggest challenge was to stay within the budget, given how much work the place needed.

WHO STOLE THE APPLIANCES?

THE WALLS AND FINISHES WERE GENERIC AND WITHOUT ANY CHARM.

THIS
PAINTING
IS BY
JAMES
SEWARD.

STEP 1

RECONSTRUCT THE STAIRCASE

The staircase is the first thing you see when you enter the house, and we needed to transform it from dark and creaky into something bold, funky, and memorable. The steps were falling apart, so we had to begin by replacing the risers and making sure the whole thing was structurally sound. When the construction was finished, the fun began. Pulling from our color scheme, we painted vertical stripes running the length of the stairs. They set the tone for the entire house, making it feel light, girly, and colorful.

THE FRIDGE IS
AS CUTE AS THE
CLIENTS.

BUILD OUT THE KITCHEN

The existing kitchen was a dark room with cheap, broken cabinets attached to the walls. There were no appliances and no useful countertops, so we started by tearing everything out. We installed white cabinetry and white subway tile to create a crisp, clean space. Inexpensive gray CaesarStone countertops brought it all together.

The light-blue 1950s retro-style refrigerator is from Smeg, and the pink stove is from BlueStar, which carries cool, vintage-looking stoves in 190 different colors. With the all-white walls and cabinetry, they combine to create an overall old-school vibe. The colors are a nod back to the striped stairs you see when you enter the house.

APPLIANCES WILL
ADD VALUE TO
ANY HOME, SO
WE SPLURGED ON
THE STOVE AND
REFRIGERATOR.

The light-blue refrigerator
and the pink stove create
an old-school vibe.

FOOD TASTES
BETTER
FROM A PINK
OVEN.

DECORATE THE LIVING ROOM

The living room walls had been painted outdated shades of brown and yellow that made the room feel small and dark. We painted them a light, subtle gray, save for one interior windowless wall that would become the focal point of the room. That was covered with hot-pink-and-silver-foil wallpaper. Anything but subtle, but that's okay because foil wallpaper is gorgeous.

A GLASS TOP DISPLAYS COLLECTIBLES.

THIS COLLAGE IS BY TONY CARAMANICO.

HOT PINK AND ROYAL BLUE PILLOWS BRING THE COUCH TO LIFE.

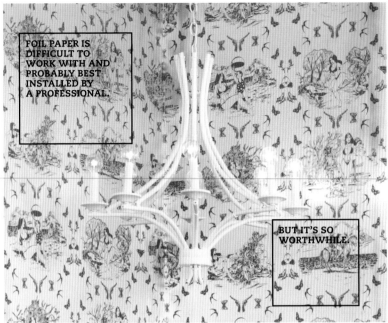

FOIL PAPER IS DIFFICULT TO WORK WITH AND PROBABLY BEST INSTALLED BY A PROFESSIONAL.

BUT IT'S SO WORTHWHILE.

SUBTLE FURNITURE COLORS BALANCE THE MANY BOLD COLORS IN THE WALLS, RUGS, AND PILLOWS.

GIRRRRRRL

Hot-pink-and-silver-foil wallpaper is anything but subtle.

ASK THE EXPERT
BETSEY JOHNSON

We asked designer Betsey Johnson about her obsession with the color pink.

Q: Why pink?
A: I was born pink, grew up pink, and constantly think pink.

Q: Why bold?
A: Because I'm a double Leo! I am only happy in bright colors.

Q: Does color make you happy?
A: Absolutely! Bright like crayon colors, like the Mickey Mouse cartoon colors! Happy, happy, happy colors! If I don't wear superbright colors, I wear black because I'm feeling lazy and want to look sophisticated.

Q: What's your least favorite color?
A: Beige! I don't like bland, boring, blah beige.

Q: What is the connection between fashion and interiors?
A: Your environment, your body— it's all the same to me! You dress your home like you dress yourself.

DESIGN A DINING SPACE

The inexpensive dining table came from Ikea, and the six metal chairs from Crate and Barrel. We added an expensive floral chair from Kartell at each end of the table to bring in color and pattern.

SPLURGE ON A PAIR OF GREAT END CHAIRS.

BEFORE:
NO POWER

AFTER:
GIRL POWER

THE ROOM NEEDED
SOME FEMININE
TOUCHES TO
SOFTEN UP THE
BOLD WALLS.

THE
CHANDELIER
ABOVE
THE BED . . .

THE WHITE
BEDDING . . .

. . . AND THE
MIRRORED END
TABLE ALL
DO SO
PERFECTLY.

STEP 5

DESIGN THE MASTER BEDROOM

The hardwood flooring in the master bedroom was rotted and falling apart. There were even sections with missing floorboards, so we had no choice but to tear it all out. We laid inexpensive wood flooring on top of the plywood subflooring, and then we stained it bright pink. If you are planning on painting new floors, you can afford to use a lower-grade hardwood, which costs a lot less.

The girls were all for taking big design risks, so we asked street artist Matt Siren to come over and work some magic. He wallpapered the room in black, white, and pink art, using wheat paste and a broom. After the graffiti was installed, he placed the large black-and-hot-pink Ghost Girl images over the walls. The girls loved it, which is why we loved the girls. They both had a huge sense of adventure when it came to design. And that is what makes what we do fun.

WHERE WE ENDED

Even when an entire place needs to be redone, you don't have to spend a fortune. Pick a theme—in this case, pink—and stick with it. A few functional design solutions transformed the dark, decrepit space into a colorful, girly, super surfer house.

A HAPPY ENTRANCE

NEUTRAL WALLS ARE THE PERFECT BACKDROP FOR BOLD ACCENTS.

THE RUG IS COZY.

HOW TO

STRIPE THE STAIRS

1. Fill all scratches and cracks with wood putty.

2. Sand the staircase.

3. Lay down a primer.

4. Paint the base coat (oil-based paint is best). In this case, the base coat was white. Let the base coat dry for at least twenty-four hours.

5. Measure out each step and mark the measurements with tape, stair by stair. After all of the steps are taped, step back to make sure they look even. Stairs can be off-kilter (staircases and walls are often uneven, especially in old houses), so your eye may work better than a measuring tape.

6. Paint the first color (stripes) all the way down. Use flat paints only.

7. Allow the paint to completely dry. Tape and paint the second color. Do the same for additional colors.

8. Coat with a commercial-grade clear polyurethane.

STAIN A HARDWOOD FLOOR

1. Fill in all cracks with wood putty.

2. Sand the floor.

3. Vacuum and mop to remove all dust particles.

4. Once the floor is dry, apply the stain.

5. Remove excess stain (after ten minutes).

6. Coat with polyurethane once the floor is fully dry.

BUDGET ANALYSIS

CONTRACTOR FEES	$26,639.00
WALLPAPER	$1,450.00
FLOORING AND CARPETS	GIFT
WINDOW TREATMENTS	$2,973.95
LIGHTING	$800.00
KITCHEN AND DINING TABLE	$4,288.18
APPLIANCES	$4,426.21
FURNITURE	$5,293.86
BEDDING	$464.00
ART	GIFT
ACCESSORIES	$120.31
TOTAL	$46,455.51

LET THERE
BE LIGHT.

Dream Duplex

Jane and David Cohen moved into their new apartment three months before we met them. The place was a spectacular three-bedroom, two-and-a-half-bathroom duplex penthouse in the Murray Hill neighborhood of Manhattan. It was brand-new and had eighteen-foot ceilings and floor-to-ceiling windows that over-looked New York City in two directions. Gorgeous.

They came to us because after three months, they had still only partially moved in. They'd hung the flat-screen TVs and unpacked their boxes, but when it came to the design and decor, they had not yet begun. In fact, they had no clue as to where to begin.

Jane and David had rented their furniture, and it was the three Bs: bad, bland, beige. The enormous white walls were empty, and

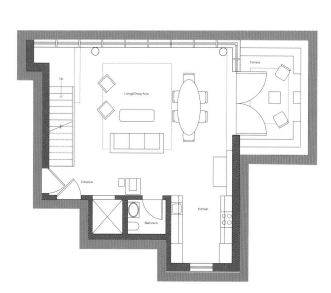

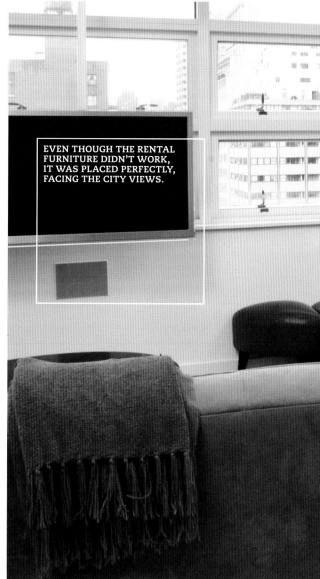

EVEN THOUGH THE RENTAL
FURNITURE DIDN'T WORK,
IT WAS PLACED PERFECTLY,
FACING THE CITY VIEWS.

there wasn't any lighting aside from the high hats in the ceilings. The Cohens had an idea of what they wanted but were unsure as to how to go about achieving it. Jane wanted a contemporary look with elegant, classical details, and she liked the idea of mixing old one-of-a-kind pieces with sleek modern design. She also knew that she wanted color and preferred blues and greens. David and Jane love to entertain, and they hoped that the apartment would become a place for friends and family to hang out and enjoy the breathtaking views.

We encounter amazing spaces all the time, and it's not uncommon if the furnishings and decor aren't up to par with the space. It's all about adding the icing on the cake.

WHERE WE STARTED

THE BUDGET
$20,000

THE GOAL
To enhance the already swoon-worthy space with color, texture, and light

THE CLIENTS' WISH LIST

1. A blue and green color palette

2. Statement-making lighting

3. Modern art

4. A mixture of vintage and modern furnishings

5. To make over the patio

PATIO WITH THAT VIEW AND NO PLACE TO SIT = A CRIME!

JANE

DAVID

STEP1
DECORATE THE LIVING AREA

All of the existing furniture had been rented, so with one phone call we were able to clear the place out and get started. We anchored the living room with a "Family" rug, one of our very own designs. The bold graphic and great message make it the perfect centerpiece for this common space, and the colors inspired the rest of the room.

We found a large cement urn at a flea market and filled it with blooming pink branches to bring in a natural touch. The crisp space sets off the urn, making it look like a gorgeous museum piece, while the urn softens the newness of the space.

THE CHAIRS AND TABLE ARE FULL OF 1950S FLAIR.

THIS SLEEK COFFEE TABLE IS FROM ADELAIDE IN THE WEST VILLAGE.

MICHAEL SMITH

Adelaide is our favorite place in New York City to purchase antiques and vintage furniture. We asked co-owner Michael Smith for his thoughts and ideas on mixing vintage and modern.

DOS AND DON'TS OF MIXING MODERN AND VINTAGE: The quality of the vintage pieces should reflect the rest of the room's decor. They should enhance what's already in the room.

RULES FOR COMBINING COLOR: You can use almost any combination of colors. What you should keep in mind is to use similar hues and intensities of color. For example, combine bright and bold colors or light and natural shades, but not both. If you want to add an accent color that strays from your overall color scheme, keep it to a single color that repeats throughout.

COMFORT VERSUS STYLE: One is not more important than the other. Comfort and style need to meet in compromise for the best results.

TIPS FOR HIGH STYLE ON A BUDGET: You can have high style on a budget if you allow a lot of time to develop your space. If you're working with a small budget, don't expect to find everything you need during a weekend at flea markets and vintage shops. Quality rooms take time to build.

The three most important factors for styling a room:

1. Find the focal point of a room. Where your eyes go when you enter a room is the focal point. Build your room around that point.
2. When building around a focal point, work from high to low. Most times this means that the focal point will be the tallest/highest point in the room. Furniture and other decor should not be higher than the focal point piece.
3. Carefully select your room's lighting.

Q: Why modern?
A: Modern gives your space a contemporary feel. You don't want your room to resemble a stage set for a period film.

Q: Why vintage?
A: The individuality of vintage pieces sets your home apart from anyone else's.

THE CANDELABRA IS FROM DUNES AND DUCHESS.

FOR A SOFTER LOOK, OVAL TABLES ARE A GREAT ALTERNATIVE TO RECTANGULAR TABLES.

THESE MISMATCHED CHAIRS WORK TOGETHER BECAUSE OF THEIR SIMILAR SHAPE.

STEP 2

DESIGN THE DINING AREA

We chose an oval table because it softens the lines of the room, while the marble feels elegant. Mixing chairs is something we do in almost every project, and we never grow tired of it. The end chairs are drastically different from the side chairs in terms of finish and color, but they are all unified through the round shape of their backs.

PICK THE ART

The wall behind the stunning staircase was enormous and screaming for a large, bold piece of art. We met with artist Cristina Vergano and commissioned her to paint something for this wall. She came back with *Figure of Speech*, a humorous and fun work that also incorporated all of Jane's favorite colors.

STAIRWAYS ARE A GREAT PLACE TO HANG ART.

THE GOLD PENDANTS ARE FROM ABC CARPET AND HOME.

STEP 4

HANG THE LIGHTS

We needed a dramatic centerpiece for the apartment, and the large pendant lights designed by Tom Dixon made a bolder statement than a chandelier would have. We hung the cluster of six pendants at different lengths so that they'd create a bigger impact and look equally stunning from above and below.

THIS IS AN OUTDOOR RUG.

STEP 5

BRING THE OUTDOORS IN AND THE INDOORS OUT

Jane and David had a great terrace but hadn't yet used it because it was empty and unfurnished. Our goal was to make it feel like part of the main room, at least during the warmer months when the doors could be left open. Our favorite part of the outdoor space is the sleek Eco Tower fireplace, which can be used inside as well. We added the metallic pillows to the green sofa to echo the metallic details inside the home.

Our goal was to make the terrace feel like part of the main room.

A HOME
BY
NOVOGRATZ

A HOME
BY
NOVOGRATZ

A HOME
BY
NOVOGRATZ

THE METALLIC PILLOWS ARE FOR COLOR AND EXTRA SEATING.

THE CITY IS
PART OF
THE ROOM.

THE COLOR
SCHEME IS
UNIFORM INSIDE
AND OUT.

The colorful "Family" rug is
our design, available at CB2.

WHERE WE ENDED

Jane and David's home was spectacular, but the bare walls and rental furniture, while temporary, did it a disservice. Art, bold lighting, and a mixture of vintage and modern furnishings complement the apartment perfectly without competing with the view for attention.

HOW TO

HANG LARGE PENDANTS AND CHANDELIERS

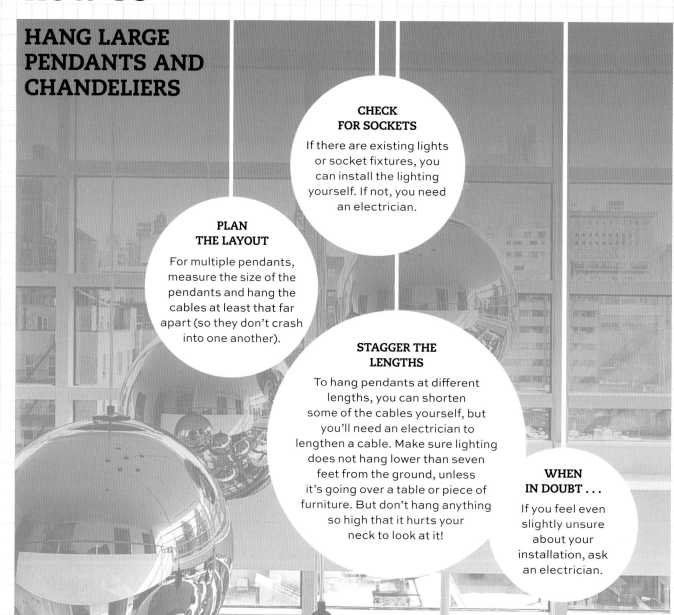

CHECK FOR SOCKETS

If there are existing lights or socket fixtures, you can install the lighting yourself. If not, you need an electrician.

PLAN THE LAYOUT

For multiple pendants, measure the size of the pendants and hang the cables at least that far apart (so they don't crash into one another).

STAGGER THE LENGTHS

To hang pendants at different lengths, you can shorten some of the cables yourself, but you'll need an electrician to lengthen a cable. Make sure lighting does not hang lower than seven feet from the ground, unless it's going over a table or piece of furniture. But don't hang anything so high that it hurts your neck to look at it!

WHEN IN DOUBT . . .

If you feel even slightly unsure about your installation, ask an electrician.

BUDGET ANALYSIS

CONTRACTOR FEES	$3,255.23
FLOORING AND CARPETS	$100.96
LIGHTING	$2,652.20
FIREPLACE	$2,830.75
FURNITURE	$7,818.15
BAR AND BAR ACCESSORIES	$528.04
PILLOWS	$818.75
ART	$517.16
BOOKS	$462.00
VASES	$1,092.98
FLOWERS	$ 2,391.76
TOTAL	$22,467.98

Suburban Basement

We met Scott and Elyse Everett and their three children, Hannah (six), Charlie (three), and Paige (six months), at their home in an upscale suburban neighborhood in New Jersey. They loved everything about the house except for the basement, which was half man cave and half playroom, completely taken over by their children's massive toy collection. This was your typical basement—dark, with brown wall-to-wall carpeting and oversized toys (think Barbie castles) strewn everywhere.

Overall, the space felt dark and uninspired, so much so that Elyse didn't even like to venture down to watch movies. The TV area was anything but chic or welcoming. The kids' side wasn't any

WHERE WE STARTED

THE GOAL
To transform a dark basement into a bright, fun hang-out space for family playtime and entertaining

THE BUDGET
$35,000

THE CLIENTS' WISH LIST

1. A bar and game area for entertaining
2. An art area for the kids
3. Art on the walls
4. Less "man cave," more style
5. New carpet

The dark, heavy furnishings made the room feel much darker than it was.

THE BROWN SOFA WAS WAY TOO HEAVY.

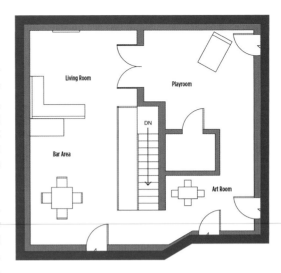

better. There was nothing on the walls, very little storage or organization, and nowhere to sit except for the floor. With the only natural light coming from a small window above the sofa, the dark, heavy furnishings, drab olive walls, and brown wall-to-wall carpeting everywhere made the room feel much darker than it was. Throughout our career, we've done very few basements. They are always a challenge—we've learned that the best solution is to make them as bright and comfortable as possible.

The Everetts craved a space that was open, clean, and clutter-free, a space in which they could spend time together as a family and also entertain friends. The basement was a large square divided into four areas: playroom, art space, TV room, and adult game area. We wanted to amplify those spaces and make them more distinct, functional, and stylish. We wanted to create a space that gave each family member an area that they could enjoy without forgoing comfort or style.

TOY EXPLOSION

REPLACE THE CARPETS

The brown wall-to-wall carpeting began at the top of the stairs, making the stairway feel like a dark tunnel that led down to a dungeon. Our first task was to get rid of it. As soon as it was gone, the space lightened up considerably (and felt far less depressing). The floors underneath were concrete, which meant we had a few options: lay new wall-to-wall carpet (too boring), install real floors (too expensive), or polish or paint the cement (too cold). We did a little research and came up with a solution: Flor carpet tiles. They look like a fun carpet, lay like tile, and can be cleaned, changed, or removed without much effort. We opted for a blue tonal checkered pattern so that the tiles wouldn't overwhelm the room.

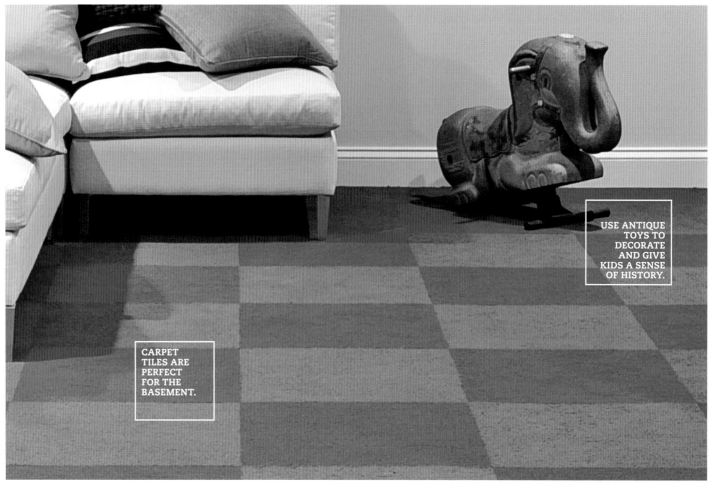

USE ANTIQUE TOYS TO DECORATE AND GIVE KIDS A SENSE OF HISTORY.

CARPET TILES ARE PERFECT FOR THE BASEMENT.

We opted for a blue tonal checkered pattern so that the tiles wouldn't overwhelm the room.

AFTER

INDIGO
VIOLET
RED
ORANGE
YELLOW
GREEN
BLUE
INDIGO
VIOLET

STEP 2
REDO THE STAIRCASE AND BUILD A SLIDE

The staircase was dark and depressing; we wanted to make the family feel they were entering a funhouse instead of a dungeon. What is more fun for a kid than entering the playroom by slide?

We constantly look to our own seven children for inspiration and fresh ideas, and entering a room via slide was definitely an idea inspired by our kids. Because the staircase was open on one side, the slide was a fairly simple addition. We cut a hole into the wall at the top of the stairs to access the slide, made a landing, and built the slide out from there (so that it would be attached to and in line with the stairs). We added a rounded edge on the open side for safety, and coated it with clear polyurethane for slipperiness. The kids were overjoyed.

We painted the stairs white and stenciled the names of the basic hues of the rainbow in their respective order on the steps. The self-adhesive vinyl stencils were custom-made by FastSigns, a company that will create and cut stencils for any design. They cost more than the nonadhesive type, but we've found that the less expensive stencils cause paint to bleed.

BEFORE

IMPROVE THE TV AREA

Scott loved the TV area, especially the projector and screen, but Elyse couldn't stand the lack of coziness and the heaviness of the space. Neither could we. The dreary green walls, the enormous brown sectional, and the furry beige carpet made the room feel dark, dated, and unwelcoming. We needed to lighten it up and bring in some color and art.

As soon as we removed the brown leather sectional, the whole space opened up. We replaced it with a modern white sofa from CB2. It's clean and sleek-looking yet still incredibly comfortable. We added an array of blue and yellow pillows for color and comfort. Pillows are a great way to add a little edge and take a risk in a space. The pillows in our own home are constantly rotating between rooms and can totally change the vibe of a space.

Like most men, Scott was very protective of his projector and screen—he didn't want them messed with or moved. So instead of changing the layout of the space, we maximized it by painting the wall behind the screen a flat black and installing a blackout shade in the window. We got rid of the glare and made the place feel like a movie theater.

THIS ART CAME FROM A WEBSITE CALLED EXHIBITION A.

SHARON MONTROSE PRINT PURCHASED ON 20x200.COM

THE LIGHT-COLORED COUCH BRIGHTENS THE ENTIRE ROOM.

ASK THE EXPERT

BILL POWERS

We asked Bill Powers, owner of Half Gallery and a judge on Bravo's *Work of Art,* for his advice on buying art online.

Q: Why do you encourage people to buy art?

A: Why buy wall decor when you can spend a little more for something that's relevant and will appreciate in value?

Q: How has the Internet affected the art world?

A: What happened to fashion in the eighties and nineties is happening with art today. People are recognizing this subculture, and they want to participate. As my friend the writer Jerry Saltz says, "You want to know how to be in the art world? Say, 'I'm in the art world!'" It's as simple as speaking a declarative sentence.

Q: Are there any cons to buying online?

A: Scale is something that's hard to gauge by numbers alone. Cut out a piece of paper according to the measurements given for a better idea of the size.

Q: Do you have any advice for anyone intimidated by the art world?

A: Literature by definition is made to educate and delight. There's no reason art can't satisfy our appetites in the same way. People can name five Real Housewives in this country but not five living artists! We need to change that.

Pillows are a great way to add a little edge.

CREATE AN
ADULT PLAY SPACE

Scott and Elyse love having friends over for drinks, poker, and movie nights. They asked us to build a bar (Scott's first request on the wish list) so that they would no longer have to run up and down the stairs for ice and beverages while they were entertaining. We knocked out the half wall at the back of the room and built a bar with a Caesar-Stone countertop in its place. We added a refrigerater, an ice maker, and a microwave to make popping popcorn while watching a movie more convenient.

PENDANTS CAN BE HUNG FROM LOW CEILINGS IF PLACED OVER A TABLE.

THIS FLAG WAS CREATED BY ARTIST ANN CARRINGTON OUT OF BOTTLE CAPS, NAILS, AND SCRAP METAL.

THE WALLPAPER IS A COLLAGE OF THE FAMILY'S PHOTOGRAPHS AND WAS PRINTED AT DUGGAL.

CREATE A GOOD-LOOKING, ORGANIZED PLAYROOM

We wanted to transform the space from a Toys "R" Us–like storage room into a place where the kids could use their imaginations, be inspired, and create.

We left the natural beige carpeting on the floors because it was neutral and our budget was limited. But an "A to Z" rug and mismatched floor pillows add color, warmth, and style to an otherwise ho-hum carpet.

The Everett kids had a ton of costumes, so we made a little corner with hooks for the hats and dress-up clothing. We added a director's chair for rehearsals and a red-and-white curtain for performances. The vintage funhouse mirror is fun for kids and adults alike (especially after they've hit the new bar!).

THIS FLEA-MARKET FIND COULD BE THE INSPIRATION FOR A BUDDING ARCHITECT.

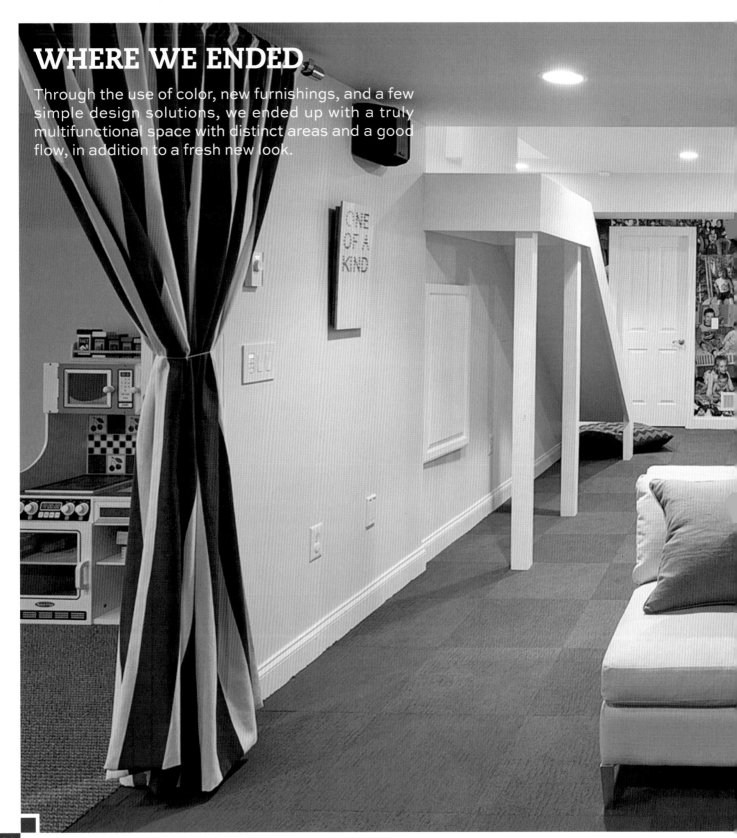

WHERE WE ENDED

Through the use of color, new furnishings, and a few simple design solutions, we ended up with a truly multifunctional space with distinct areas and a good flow, in addition to a fresh new look.

ONE
OF A
KIND

CUSTOMIZE YOUR OWN FAMILY PHOTO WALLPAPER AT DUGGAL IN NEW YORK.

THIS MIRROR IS FROM ADELAIDE, A VINTAGE STORE IN NEW YORK.

HOW TO

INSTALL CARPET TILES

PULL UP OLD CARPET
Remove the carpet and all the underlayer until all that remains is the plywood or concrete.

ADD CORK
(OPTIONAL)
Add a layer of cork if you need soundproofing or would like a softer floor. Use glue to attach the cork to the floor, or the carpet tiles will move.

PREPARE THE FLOOR
Vacuum and scrub the floor and allow it to dry.

LAY THE TILES
There are arrows on the back of each tile. Make sure that all arrows point in the same direction, whether you are using patterns or solids.

STENCIL A STAIRCASE

VIOLET
RED
ORANGE
YELLOW
GREEN
BLUE
INDIGO

SAND THE ENTIRE STAIRCASE
Fill all cracks and holes with a putty knife, then sand the staircase in the same direction as the grain with a fine-grit sanding pad. When you're finished, vacuum the dirt and dust.

PAINT A LAYER OF PRIMER
Using a small roller or a flat brush, paint a coat of high-quality oil-based primer over the stairs.

PAINT THE BASE COAT
For the stairs, use either oil paint or latex, but never a semigloss, because the stencils will peel off the paint and the edges around the stenciling will crack. Flat paints are best.

CREATE YOUR LAYOUT
After the base coat has dried, measure one step and decide where to place the stencil (if in the middle, measure from each side as well as from the top and bottom). Mark with a pencil.

APPLY THE STENCILS
Peel and stick the stencil (leave pencil marks exposed so that they will be painted over).

PAINT INSIDE THE STENCILS
Use a flat paint for the same reasons as above. Spray paints work well with stencils.

REMOVE THE STENCILS
Adhesive stencils will peel off without smudging the paint, even if the paint is still damp. Start from one corner and slowly peel the stencil back, removing it from the surface.

APPLY A POLY COAT
Add a clear coat of polyurethane to the entire staircase. It will keep the stenciling sharp and the steps clean.

BUDGET ANALYSIS

	CONTRACTOR FEES	$13,285.00
	PHOTO WALLPAPER	$2,177.50
	FLOORING AND CARPETS	$2,428.86
	WINDOW AND DOOR TREATMENTS	$648.10
	LIGHTING	$1,197.60
	FURNITURE	$4,895.58
	APPLIANCES	$4,228.66
	CUSTOM SLIDE	$1,575.00
	ART	$1,346.34
	ART SUPPLIES AND STORAGE	$1,124.60
	ACCESSORIES	$4,467.60
	YOGA MATS AND EXERCISE BALLS	$168.94
	TOTAL	**$37,543.78**

Model Home

One Management asked us if we could create a home away from home for four up-and-coming models who had recently arrived in New York. The women, who were sharing bedrooms and bathrooms in a small apartment in Brooklyn, were from four different countries, and each was a stranger to the others. The apartment was a revolving door—when one model left, another moved in. Some stayed a few weeks, and others, months.

Because we've moved numerous times and have often had to vacate one home before the next place was ready, we've lived in our fair share of temporary spaces—some for a few weeks and some for as long as six or seven months. For the sake of the kids and because we never know for certain how long we'll need to

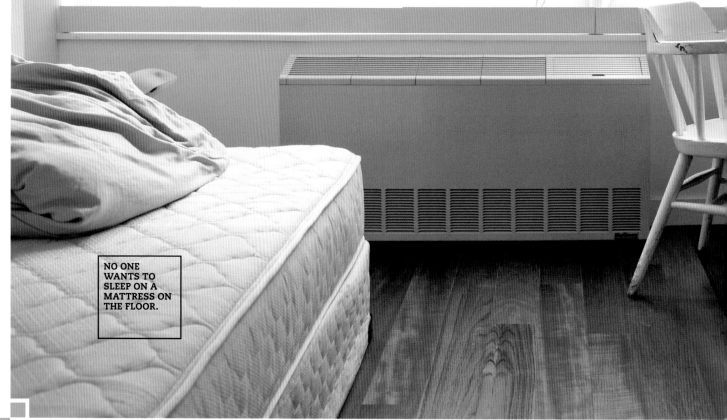

WHERE WE STARTED

THE GOAL

To create a space that feels like a home—even if it's only home for a short while

THE BUDGET

$20,000

THE CLIENT'S WISH LIST

1. To bring in color and personality

2. A more functional kitchen

3. A boutique hotel vibe

4. New furniture

5. Art on the walls

6. Lighting

PROPER WINDOW TREATMENTS ARE A MUST— ESPECIALLY FOR YOUNG MODELS WHO NEED THEIR BEAUTY SLEEP.

NO ONE WANTS TO SLEEP ON A MATTRESS ON THE FLOOR.

DINING AREA OR INTERROGATION ROOM?

The bedrooms looked like dorm rooms.

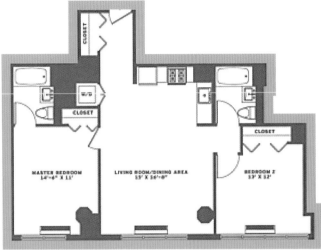

stay, we have always made it a priority to make each of these temporary spaces feel like a home. We move in, decorate, and treat the space as if we'll be there forever. And that is exactly what we wanted to do with this place.

When we arrived, the apartment was bleak at best. It was a white box with zero charm. The living and dining areas didn't look like they had ever been lived or dined in; they were really just a pathway to the bedrooms. The white walls were empty, and the few pieces of existing furniture were drab and depressing. The bedrooms looked like dorm rooms, only *after* the students had left for the summer, with a couple of mattresses on the floor and cheap wooden dressers set against the wall. The apartment needed color, light, personality, and a few unique design solutions to create a livable situation. It was a rental, so changes in construction were not an option. Our aim was to maximize the space by adding cozy furniture, cool vintage lighting, and art and wallpaper on the bare white walls to give it the look of a boutique hotel—sleek and clean—and at the same time to create a space that was warm and comfortable.

CREATE A MORE FUNCTIONAL KITCHEN

The kitchen was open to the living room and had new finishes, cabinets, and appliances, but it lacked counter space, storage, and light. To make it more inviting and—more important—functional, we bought a used industrial kitchen cart from a restaurant supply shop on the Bowery in Manhattan. It gives the kitchen a much-needed extra countertop and additional storage. It also serves to divide the kitchen from the living and dining area. Lastly, we added some flowers, which make any space come alive.

Flowers make any space come alive.

THE TWO RED PENDANT LAMPS BRING IN BOTH COLOR AND LIGHT.

DESPERATELY NEEDED EXTRA STORAGE AND COUNTER SPACE

CHANDELIERS
CAN HANG FROM
A LOW CEILING
IF PLACED
STRATEGICALLY,
LIKE IN A CORNER
OR ABOVE A PIECE
OF FURNITURE.

STEP 2

LIGHT THE LIVING ROOM

We found a gorgeous vintage chandelier at Bowery Lighting Co. that we knew would give the living room a homey yet glamorous feel, while also adding a sense of history to the brand-new apartment. It would have hung too low if we had placed it in the center of the room (especially in an apartment full of very tall women), so we had to come up with an alternate plan. We chose to hang it in the corner, highlighting the gorgeous wallpaper and sofa, and with no risk of bumping one's head on it. We brought in additional light through a floor lamp and a table lamp.

THIS PIECE IS BY ARTIST JAMISON ERNEST.

THE SUPERMODEL IN ALL OF US NEEDS A FULL-LENGTH MIRROR.

TWO NEW CHAIRS FROM CB2 WERE ADDED TO THE EXISTING ONES FROM KARTELL.

FURNISH THE LIVING AND DINING AREA

With almost no furniture and nothing on the walls, the living and dining area felt more like a hallway than somewhere to hang out. And that is exactly how it had been used—as a place to pass through on the way to a bathroom or a bedroom. Because the women didn't know one another, it was easy for them to ignore the fact that there was a space in the middle of their apartment built for shared living. We wanted to create a warm and homey area where they would feel comfortable spending time together and entertaining friends.

We got rid of the generic white table and replaced it with a hip round chartreuse table. We kept the two white ghost chairs from Kartell and brought in two others. Mixed chairs—vintage with modern, high-end with low—make any table look more interesting and less serious, providing instant cool. When everything matches perfectly, a room can look as if it was copied straight from a catalog (and feel just like everyone else's). We decorated the table with five silver candlesticks in all different shapes and sizes, adding some girly elegance and charm to the room.

The living area felt like a doctor's waiting room. It was nearly empty aside from an old, flimsy blue couch and a cheap wooden end table. The lighting situation added to the dreariness; other than the track lights in the ceiling, there was only one small table lamp next to the sofa.

SSSSHHHH.

When everything matches perfectly, a room can look as if it was copied straight from a catalog.

THIS SOFA CAME FROM ETSY.

THE VINTAGE RUG BRINGS OUT THE BLUE ACCENTS IN THE PILLOWS AND WALLPAPER.

THE BLUE FLOWER DETAIL PULLS THE APARTMENT TOGETHER BY TYING INTO THE FLORAL DETAILS ON THE PAPERS IN THE BEDROOMS.

HANGING WALLPAPER IS NOT EASY; CONSIDER HIRING A PROFESSIONAL.

STEP 4

CREATE A WALL OF FAME

To create the black-and-white model wall, we brought all of the head shots from One Management's portfolio to Flavor Paper, a custom wallpaper company in Brooklyn. They took the photographs and transformed them into stunning wallpaper. For color, we asked them to add bright blue flower accents throughout the design. The blue flower accents help to make the whole apartment feel cohesive, as all three of the wallpapers used have different blue flowers.

FURNISH THE BEDROOMS

The apartment has two bedrooms, and two women share each one. However, none of the models really had a space to call her own.

Our task was to make the rooms feel comfortable enough that the women would actually unpack, move in, and feel at home. We purchased four inexpensive bed frames at Ikea and four sets of white sheets, pillowcases, and duvets at Bed Bath and Beyond. The new beds and bedding immediately transformed the spaces from dorm rooms to something you'd find in a boutique hotel.

We got rid of the brown dressers and installed drawers and inexpensive storage in the closets, both to create more space in the rooms themselves and to give each woman a private place to keep her things.

THE PILLOWCASE PICKS UP A COLOR IN THE WALLPAPER.

HAND-SILK-SCREENED WALLPAPER TURNS THIS INTO A FOCAL WALL.

ASK THE EXPERT
JON SHERMAN

Jon Sherman is the founder and head designer of Flavor Paper, a hip, high-end wall-covering and design company based in Brooklyn. We asked him for some insider tips on using wallpaper.

Q: Why use wallpaper?

A: Wallpaper has a vastly more dramatic effect than paint. Color can affect mood, but you can incorporate that color into your wallpaper and get the same effect, with the added benefit of pattern. In many circumstances, the ability to steer a room toward a desired vibe cannot be accomplished with anything but wallpaper. You can open up a world of wonder and intrigue with well-chosen wallpaper.

Q: Give us some tips for choosing colors and patterns.

A: Color is a very personal decision, but choosing something you really love, and will love for a long time, is important. Make sure the color will work within an existing color scheme, or use the color to determine the palette. We always recommend using silver and chrome. They pick up all of the colors in the room, and there's no need to change the wallpaper when you've redecorated with a new color scheme.

Pattern is also a very personal choice, but opt for a pattern that is reflective of the style of the rest of the home. Scale can dramatically change the feel of the room, and the interaction of pattern and color will also impact the overall effect. Go with a pattern that will outlast trends or changes of heart. Pick something you feel is timeless, and it will never grow old.

Wallpaper has a vastly more dramatic effect than paint.

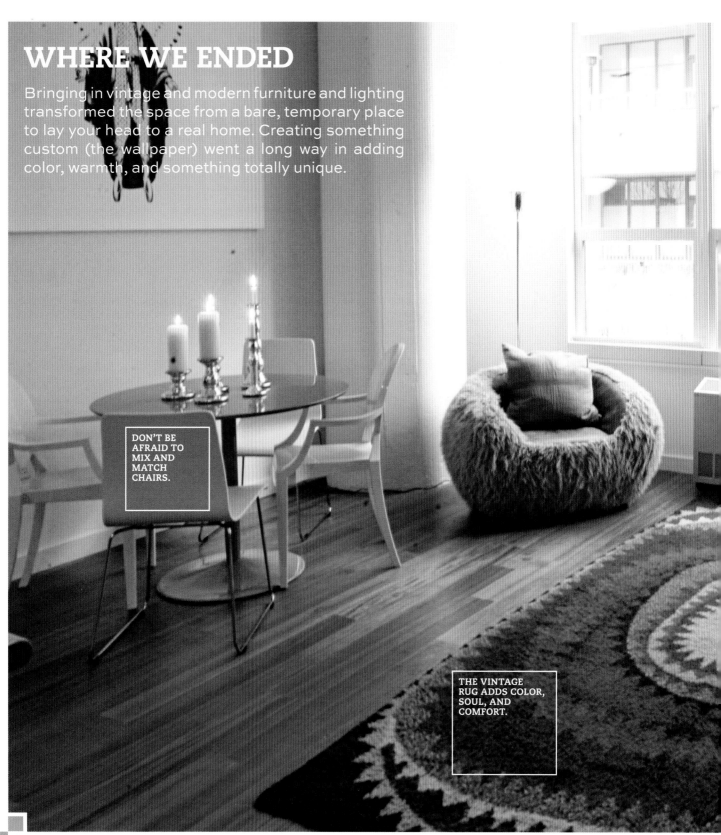

WHERE WE ENDED

Bringing in vintage and modern furniture and lighting transformed the space from a bare, temporary place to lay your head to a real home. Creating something custom (the wallpaper) went a long way in adding color, warmth, and something totally unique.

DON'T BE AFRAID TO MIX AND MATCH CHAIRS.

THE VINTAGE RUG ADDS COLOR, SOUL, AND COMFORT.

THE CHANDELIER
IS IN THE CORNER
SO THE TALL
MODELS DON'T
BUMP THEIR
HEADS.

HOW TO

HANG WALLPAPER

PREPARE THE WALLS
Prime the walls with wallpaper primer only.

GATHER YOUR TOOLS
Before you begin installation, have all supplies on hand: wallpaper, paste, knives or razor blades, sponges, rulers, and brushes (it can be disastrous if the paste starts to dry while you are still running around looking for a brush).

CUT THE PAPER
Always cut the paper too long, so that there is excess at the floor and ceiling. Cut the excess off after the paper has been applied.

CHECK THE PASTE
There are different types of wallpaper, and each requires a specific type of paste. Make certain your paste is right for your paper.

KEEP IT CLEAN
While hanging wallpaper, wash the paste off continuously—wipe the paper with a damp sponge to remove all paste and air bubbles.

STOP! AND HIRE A PROFESSIONAL!
We've tried to hang wallpaper ourselves before, and trust us, we learned the hard way never to do it again.

REWIRE A VINTAGE LAMP

Begin by taking apart the original lamp. Most floor lamps are threaded pipe screwed together. Unscrew the base and work your way up the lamp. After you've done this, insert the wire and thread it through from the base up to the socket. Then add the socket and attach the new socket with small wire nuts. The red wire goes to hot and the black goes to neutral. Put it back together. Screw the threaded pipes together, working your way down to the base of the lamp.

BUDGET ANALYSIS

	CONTRACTOR FEES	$5,500.00
	WALLPAPER	$3,707.11
	FLOORING AND CARPETS	$900.00
	LIGHTING	$2,389.45
	FURNITURE	$4,499.74
	MIRROR WALL	$675.00
	BEDDING	$365.54
	ELECTRONICS	$87.05
	ART	$3,816.00
	TOTAL	**$21,939.89**

Beach Condo

Dave and Kyra Barry have been friends of ours for more than a decade. We've designed numerous spaces for them, including Bungalow, their boutique hotel in Long Branch, New Jersey. They are every designer's dream client—fun, adventurous, and eager to push the envelope. They've owned a condo next door to the hotel for years, but they never got around to decorating it. It's a large three-bedroom, three-bathroom apartment with incredible views of the ocean. When they asked us to take over, it looked exactly the same as it had when they first moved in. It was sparsely furnished with dark, dated furniture and carpeted throughout with beige wall-to-wall. There was nothing on the walls and only the bare essentials in terms of decor. It looked and felt

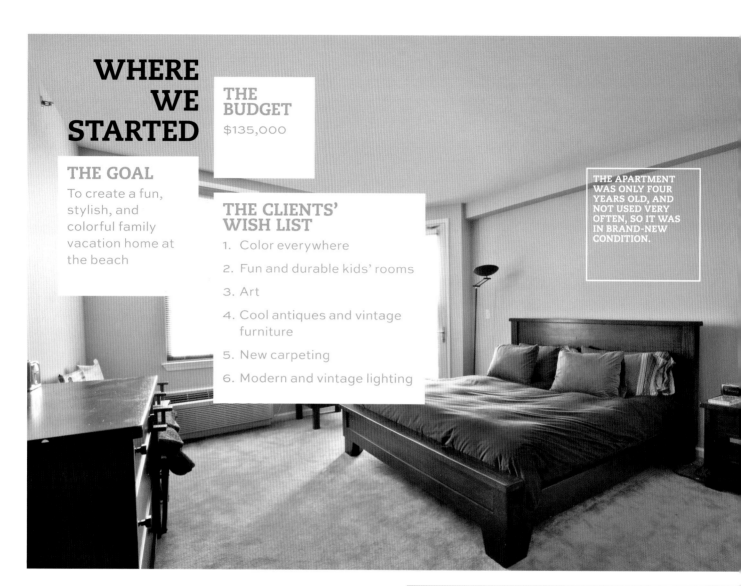

WHERE WE STARTED

THE BUDGET

$135,000

THE GOAL

To create a fun, stylish, and colorful family vacation home at the beach

THE CLIENTS' WISH LIST

1. Color everywhere
2. Fun and durable kids' rooms
3. Art
4. Cool antiques and vintage furniture
5. New carpeting
6. Modern and vintage lighting

THE APARTMENT WAS ONLY FOUR YEARS OLD, AND NOT USED VERY OFTEN, SO IT WAS IN BRAND-NEW CONDITION.

TOO DRAB

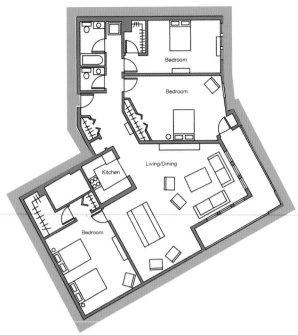

a lot like corporate housing—the opposite of what a vacation home should feel like. The place drained the energy out of anyone who walked through the front door. All in all, it was a white shell with spectacular views.

The Barrys wanted the condo to become a true escape with tons of color and life. The best part of designing a vacation home is that you can afford to take bigger risks and make bolder design choices, because it's only used so many times a year and not something you have to live with day to day.

Our goal was to add vibrant, loud, bold colors to every inch of the apartment. We wanted to transform the space from black-and-white to color, just like in *The Wizard of Oz*.

NO WINDOW TREATMENTS, AND BORING FURNITURE THAT DIDN'T GO WELL TOGETHER

REPLACE THE CARPETING

Our first task was to get rid of the beige wall-to-wall carpeting. We would have loved to lay hardwood flooring, but because it was a condo, we had to follow some rules: all of the apartments in the building had to be carpeted and soundproofed. Instead of installing new wall-to-wall, we laid Flor carpet tiles throughout the entire place, using different colors and patterns in each room.

For soundproofing, we glued a layer of cork on top of the plywood and then installed the carpet tiles onto the cork. The cork layer also adds cushioning and creates a softer floor than carpet tile installed directly onto plywood. The tiles add a ton of color and are the best alternative to wall-to-wall that we know of. Each piece can be individually removed, cleaned, or replaced if it's spilled on or stained—which is a huge bonus, especially for people with kids or pets.

CARPET TILES ARE AVAILABLE IN EVERY COLOR AND PATTERN IMAGINABLE.

WE FOUND THE WALLPAPER AT MATTER, A DESIGN STORE IN SOHO.

STEP 2

DECORATE THE WALLS

To create an old-school Palm Beach feel, we went crazy with the walls and used a combination of black-and-white wallpaper and sea-green paint throughout the living space. The paper we used is from Tres Tintas and is called Revival Almendro. It's elegant and unexpected and pops against the bright wall color. Because it's such a bold pattern and a small amount creates a huge statement, we kept it to the foyer and one small wall in the dining room.

We used a combination of shades and drapes for the windows to satisfy our needs for both form and function. The drapes add elegance and bring style to the space, while the shades are merely functional, because it's so bright at the beach.

THE ENTRYWAY

Entryways and foyers exist as places to remove coats and shoes, set keys and bags down, and welcome whoever is walking through the front door, setting the mood for the rest of the home.

We got rid of the heavy console and brought in a crazy marble table. We sanded the legs and painted them the same sea green as the walls—only with high-gloss paint, making the table a kind of foreshadowing of the color explosion in the rest of the apartment.

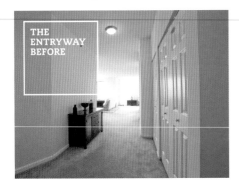

THE ENTRYWAY BEFORE

THIS LAMP LOOKS LIKE A MODERN DISCO BALL.

THE ENTRYWAY AFTER

THE PAINT COLOR IS RUMMY FROM OUR NOVOGRATZ FOR STARK PAINT LINE.

DECORATE THE LIVING ROOM

Aside from the yellow sofa from CB2, all of the furniture in the living room is vintage. The black sofa and oversized black ottoman came from Regan and Smith, an antiques store in Hudson, New York. The antique pieces are old-school elegant, and the yellow sofa adds color. We purchased the two 1950s slipper chairs at Adelaide in Manhattan. They're more subtle than the rest of the furniture, but their pale colors and funky shape add character and charm. The gold-wire end tables, also from Adelaide, are classic 1960s, in a ritzy way.

VINTAGE

THESE CUSTOM-MADE PILLOWS BRING ALL THE COLORS IN THE ROOM TOGETHER.

VINTAGE

Aside from the yellow sofa from CB2, all of the furniture in the living room is vintage.

THE ORANGE PENDANT PLAYS OFF THE COLORS IN THE LIGHT BOXES.

THE KIDS FELL IN LOVE WITH THESE OVERSIZED CHAIRS.

BENCHES DON'T CLUTTER UP A SPACE THE WAY EXTRA CHAIRS WOULD.

STEP 5

REDO THE DINING ROOM

We found the huge wood Big Sur dining table and benches at Crate and Barrel. It accommodates the Barrys' family of five with plenty of extra seating for guests. Benches are intimate but can also hold a lot of people, which makes them the perfect choice for a vacation home.

Artist Heidi Cody created the "Family" light boxes with letters from well-known brands and logos. They work especially well above the dining table, where the family usually congregates. We love light boxes—not only do they look modern and chic, but they also bring a ton of color and light to any space.

REDO LIVI'S BEDROOM

Livi, the Barrys' sixteen-year-old daughter, asked for a pink room. Her wish was our command—maybe more than she imagined. We gave her pink walls, pink floors, pink pillows, a pink throw, and a pink screen above the bed.

We replaced her bed with an inexpensive one from Ikea and covered it with white bedding; a combination of custom, store-bought, and vintage pillows; and a vintage throw. The screen above the bed is a Space Curtain, designed in the 1970s by Paco Rabanne. Have fun and think outside the box (or frame) when it comes to art.

THIS PAINT COLOR IS HOLLEDER PUNCH FROM OUR NOVOGRATZ FOR STARK PAINT LINE.

EVERY GIRL LOVES SOME BLING.

THE LOW HEADBOARD ALLOWS MORE ROOM FOR ART.

COZY AND
HIP GAETANO
PESCE
POLTRONA
CHAIR

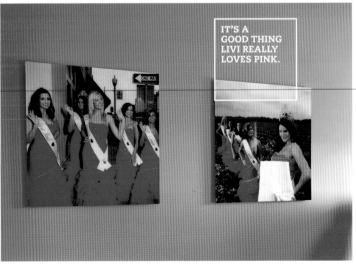

IT'S A
GOOD THING
LIVI REALLY
LOVES PINK.

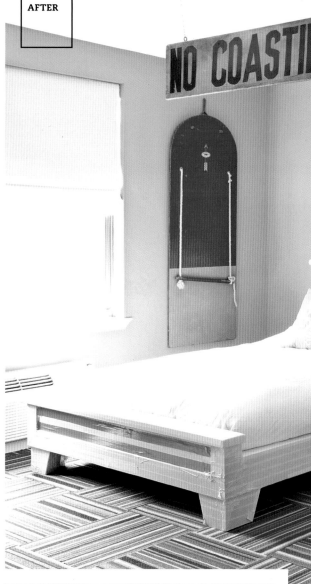

STEP 7

REDO JAKE AND CHARLIE'S BEDROOM

When we asked the Barrys' sons, Jake and Charlie, what their number one request for their room was, Jake said, "Durability." That was a new one for us, but it made us think—instead of getting rid of the heavy, dark beds, why not cover them in red, white, and blue duct tape. The result was two colorful striped beds that are extra durable.

Although there is a lot going on in this space, the blue walls and colorful beds and carpet all play off one another. We found the vintage boogie board and the NO COASTING sign at Paula Rubenstein in SoHo. Traditional art is fantastic, but don't limit yourself—there are so many other things that can be hung on the walls. The boogie board gives the room the old-school beach look we were hoping to achieve.

BEFORE

LOOKS LIKE A HOLIDAY INN CIRCA 1972

OWN HILL

THE NO COASTING DOWN HILL SIGN AND VINTAGE BOOGIE BOARD CAME FROM PAULA RUBENSTEIN IN MANHATTAN.

HANGING ART ABOVE HEADBOARDS IS A GREAT WAY TO DESIGNATE WHOSE BED IS WHOSE, AND IT CARRIES YOUR EYE UP TO THE CEILING.

THE PAINT COLOR IS BELL AMY BLUE FROM OUR NOVOGRATZ FOR STARK PAINT LINE.

TILES: UPS AND DOWNS BY FLOR

Dave and Kyra told us to go crazy with color,
and we didn't want to let them down.

THE LOVE SHACK SIGN WAS CUSTOM MADE, AND FOR ADDED HUMOR, WE HUNG A MIRROR ON THE CEILING.

THE VINTAGE
LAMPS ARE
IDENTICAL,
WHICH WORKS
BECAUSE THE
BEDSIDE TABLES
DON'T MATCH.

THE THROW
IS VINTAGE,
WHICH IS JUST
WHAT THIS
HEAVY BROWN
BED NEEDED.

TILES:
RAKE ME
OVER
BY FLOR

STEP 8

RECONCEIVE THE MASTER BEDROOM

Dave and Kyra told us to go crazy with color, and we didn't want to let them down. The yellow we chose for their room probably made it the brightest room in all of Long Branch. The existing bed was fine to keep—it anchored the room, and a little dark was good against the yellow walls.

The vintage political posters were inexpensive but look spectacular in the wood frames. For a bonus, we filled the big shell beneath the posters with sunglasses, just in case the room gets too bright.

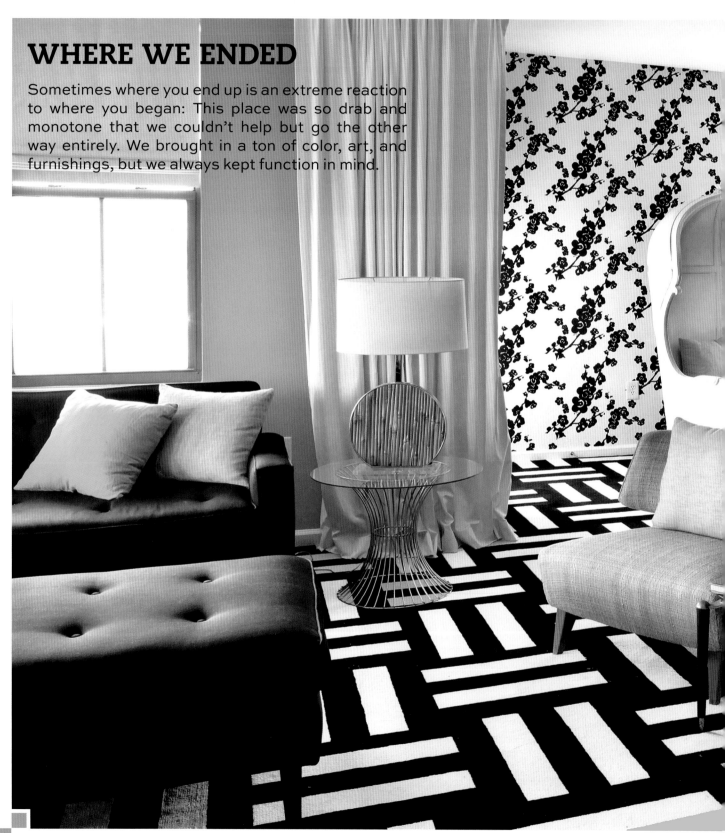

WHERE WE ENDED

Sometimes where you end up is an extreme reaction to where you began: This place was so drab and monotone that we couldn't help but go the other way entirely. We brought in a ton of color, art, and furnishings, but we always kept function in mind.

BRIGHT ORANGE LAMPS ARE ALSO VERY HAPPY.

YELLOW PILLOWS ARE HAPPY PILLOWS.

HOW TO

PAINT A ROOM

CHOOSING A COLOR
Light is a major factor when selecting a color. Prior to making your final selection, paint a piece of paper or board and observe how the color changes depending upon the time of day or light source.

THERE ARE NO RULES
Options abound. You can choose colored walls with white woodwork, one color for walls and woodwork, or light walls and darker woodwork. Whichever way you go, it's your own personal canvas; it should reflect you and how you live.

USE HIGH-QUALITY BRUSHES OR ROLLERS
Less expensive brushes shed bristles. Long bristles can apply too much paint, resulting in sags and drips. Long-handled rollers work well when painting walls and ceilings. They provide for the smooth, even application of all finishes.

SURFACE PREPARATION
The degree of preparation, whether it's cleaning, sanding, or stripping, will depend upon the job. The ultimate quality of the finish will be determined by the care taken in the preparation. Use a solution of a mild, powdered detergent and water if a preliminary washing is required. Liquid cleaners tend to leave a film, which will interfere with proper adhesion.

PRIMER OR UNDERCOAT
Although it may not always be necessary, the application of an appropriate primer or undercoat significantly enhances the coverage, appearance, and durability of paint finishes. It provides the foundation to ensure the perfect surface for bonding.

SAND BETWEEN COATS
Professional painters sand lightly with a fine sand paper (220 to 320 grit) between coats to produce a high-quality sheen. Sanding maximizes adhesion and eliminates surface imperfections. On walls and ceilings, this may be accomplished easily with a conventional pole sander. Walls and ceilings should then be vacuumed or wiped prior to applying the next coat of paint; woodwork should be vacuumed or wiped as well.

BUDGET ANALYSIS

CONTRACTOR FEES	$15,671.75
WALLPAPER	$1,516.25
FLOORING AND CARPETS	$10,441.69
WINDOW TREATMENTS	$9,465.08
LIGHTING	$4,674.50
FURNITURE	$24,340.45
BEDDING	$947.46
ART	$42,394.57
SPACE CURTAIN	$3,000.00
ACCESSORIES	$ 18,467.19
MISCELLANEOUS	$ 2,106.46
TOTAL	**$133,025.40**

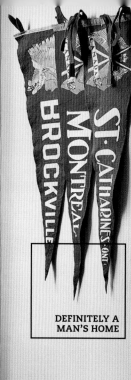

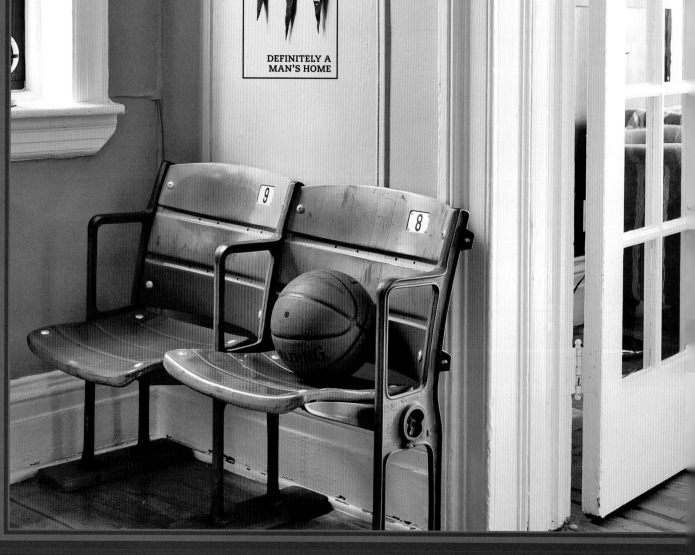

ST·CATHARINES·ONT·
MONTREAL
BROCKVILLE

DEFINITELY A
MAN'S HOME

Village Railroad

Dave Crisanti has been a good friend of ours for decades and had come to us for help with the design of his rental apartment, a large three-bedroom, one-bathroom in a prewar building in New York City's East Village. The place is gorgeous, with high ceilings, beautiful moldings, and tons of intricate detailing. The three main rooms—a bedroom, a living room, and another living room that doubled as an office—were all spacious, white, and filled with a hodgepodge of furnishings and personal items, none of which fit the space or Dave's style and taste. Since the apartment is a rental, Dave didn't want to invest too much time or money. But that philosophy is what made it feel like a temporary space filled with random furniture, a few pieces of art, and a lot of clutter.

WHERE WE STARTED

THE BUDGET
$14,000

THE GOAL
To transform a rental apartment into a home

THE CLIENT'S WISH LIST
1. New paint
2. A dining area
3. To incorporate existing antiques into new design
4. Personalization
5. Reconfigured rooms

THE DARK BOOKSHELVES WERE TOO BULKY FOR THE SPACE.

Every place you live in should feel like a home—even if it's for the very short term.

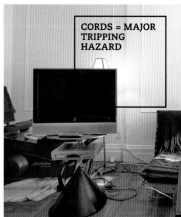

CORDS = MAJOR TRIPPING HAZARD

Our plan was to redefine the rooms, giving him a "real" living room, a dining room, and a new bedroom; get rid of a ton of the unnecessary furniture and belongings; and turn Dave's place into a home.

We often hear people say they don't want to commit to or invest in a rental if they don't know whether they'll be there for six or even two years, but the truth is people usually end up staying a lot longer than they expect to. We believe that every place you live in should feel like a home—even if it's for the very short term.

FUTONS WORK—IN COLLEGE.

IF YOU'RE GOING TO KEEP YOUR CLOTHING OUT IN THE OPEN, FOLD IT NEATLY.

THE NEW, STREAMLINED BOOKSHELVES DON'T OVERWHELM THE SPACE.

THE TV LOOKS BETTER ON THIS VINTAGE DRESSER.

PAINTING IS AN INEXPENSIVE WAY TO MAKE A RENTAL FEEL LIKE A REAL HOME.

STEP 1
REPAINT

The entire apartment had beautiful prewar moldings, baseboards, and architectural details, but they disappeared into the stark-white walls. We brought a different color into each of the three rooms, defining each space and highlighting the architectural details that make Dave's apartment so unique and special.

In the master bedroom, we painted the wall behind the bed dark green and left the other three walls white, so the room would remain bright and open. The green wall became the focal wall, a great place to show off the new vintage bed and some art.

We painted the middle room, which was to become the dining area and bar, a light gray—elegant and appropriate for the mid-century modern vibe we were trying to achieve.

The living room is large and gets fantastic light, so we could get away with painting it a deep blue.

OVERLAPPING
THE RUGS
ADDS TEXTURE
AND DEPTH.

DESIGN THE LIVING ROOM

The second living room was a combination office and TV area. The furniture didn't fit the space, wires were sticking out from the TV, and there was clutter throughout.

We kept Dave's desk but got rid of the black office chair that looked like it had been stolen from a 1980s boardroom. We replaced the clutter on the desktop with a few vintage items, like the pencil holder, vase, and horse-head bookends. Over the years, Dave had collected many antique rugs from around the world, so we pulled out five of the most interesting ones and made one large rug by overlapping them.

We removed the old furniture and brought in a gray-and-white-striped sofa and club chairs. The large sofa cushion was reupholstered in the same shade of blue that we used on the walls.

THE PRINCETON ARTWORK IS BY TERRY ROSEN (PRINCETON IS DAVE'S ALMA MATER).

The entire apartment had beautiful prewar moldings.

DESIGN THE DINING AREA AND BAR

This room had been the "main" living room, but we needed to create a proper dining space out of one of the two living rooms. Because of its proximity to the kitchen, we chose the middle room for the dining area and bar.

The dining table that Dave had in storage fit the room perfectly. The metal chairs came from an antiques store in Palm Beach. We had snatched them up on a trip a few months back and had been waiting for the perfect space to use them in. On the wall across from the dining table, we created a bar and a small seating area. The club chairs from CB2 have an old-school look and style. The antique cabinet is a gorgeous piece that Dave owned—but it had gotten lost amid the hodgepodge of furniture. Transforming it into a bar and placing it between the club chairs allowed it to be seen and appreciated again.

AN ANTIQUE CURIO CABINET IS THE PERFECT SHOWCASE FOR DAVE'S COLLECTION OF CONCERT TICKETS.

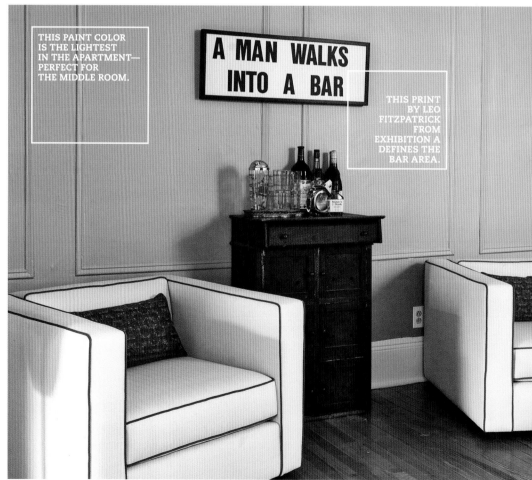

THIS PAINT COLOR IS THE LIGHTEST IN THE APARTMENT—PERFECT FOR THE MIDDLE ROOM.

A MAN WALKS INTO A BAR

THIS PRINT BY LEO FITZPATRICK FROM EXHIBITION A DEFINES THE BAR AREA.

BEFORE

THIS MIDCENTURY CHANDELIER IS FROM HOLLER AND SQUALL, A VINTAGE STORE IN BROOKLYN.

THIS COLORFUL PIECE IS BY ARTIST MARC DENNIS.

WE HAD THESE VINTAGE CHAIRS REUPHOLSTERED TO BRIGHTEN UP THE TABLE.

WE HAD DAVE'S OLD PRINCETON SWEATER FRAMED IN THIS CUSTOM SHADOW BOX.

THE VINTAGE BED ADDS COLOR AND INTEREST BUT IS STILL APPROPRIATELY MASCULINE.

STEP 4

DESIGN THE MASTER BEDROOM

Dave's bedroom was in dire need of an overhaul. In addition to a cheap wooden bed, he had mismatched tapestries covering the French doors, and piles of clothing spilling off his open metal shelves.

We fell in love with this vintage bed while we were working on a project in Oklahoma. It was incredibly inexpensive, so we shipped it home, knowing we'd use it on another job. Dave's place was the perfect fit. We replaced the bedding with high-end sheets, pillows, and a duvet from ABC Carpet and Home. Great bedding can transform any bed into a luxurious haven.

To create more room, we changed the layout by moving the bed closer to the windows, centered on the green wall. That made enough space to bring in a wardrobe and get rid of the metal shelves. Beat-up white curtains were replaced by simple and inexpensive dark panels that add a masculine touch and some texture.

The French doors that separated the bedroom from the dining room were stunning—but hidden under oversized tapestries. Lace panels show off the doors, add a soft touch, and let in some light while still offering privacy.

LACE PANELS SHOW OFF THE FRENCH DOORS AND ADD A SOFT TOUCH TO THE VERY MASCULINE ROOM.

THE DARK PAINT HIGHLIGHTS THE MOLDING AND DETAILS.

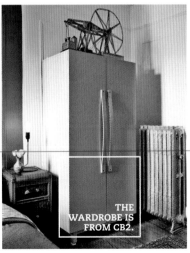

THE WARDROBE IS FROM CB2.

We changed the
layout by moving
the bed closer
to the windows.

WHERE WE ENDED

By giving each of the three main rooms a distinct purpose and personality with color, art, lighting, and furnishings, we were able to create a better flow throughout the apartment and to make the rental unit feel like a permanent home.

THIS PHOTO IS CALLED *COCKPIT.* IT'S FROM ROOM 125.

THESE STRIPED PILLOWS WERE CUSTOM MADE. THEY LIGHTEN UP THE SOFA.

THE BOLD
COLOR IS
MASCULINE
BUT WARM.

THESE
INEXPENSIVE
WINDOW
TREATMENTS
(FROM BED BATH
AND BEYOND)
ARE PERFECT FOR
A RENTAL.

THE VINTAGE
LEATHER EAMES
OFFICE CHAIR
CAME FROM
CRAIGSLIST.

PLAID—A
MASCULINE
TOUCH

HOW TO
LAYER RUGS

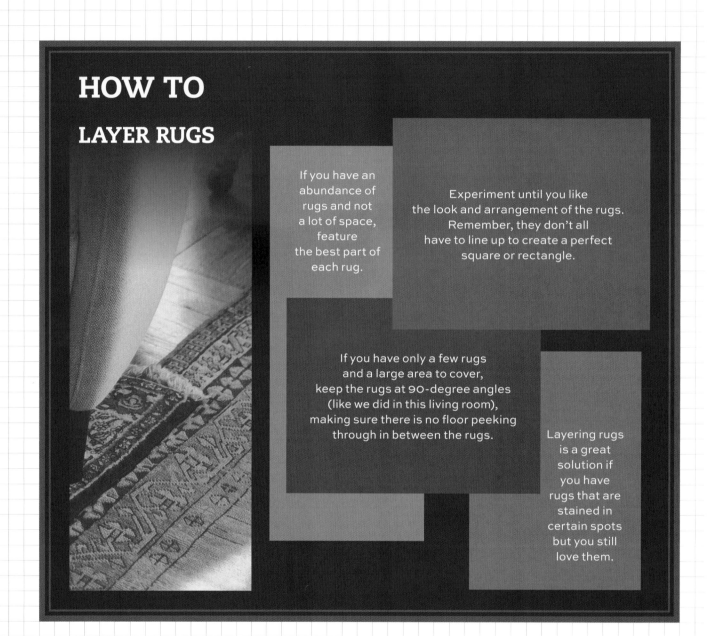

If you have an abundance of rugs and not a lot of space, feature the best part of each rug.

Experiment until you like the look and arrangement of the rugs. Remember, they don't all have to line up to create a perfect square or rectangle.

If you have only a few rugs and a large area to cover, keep the rugs at 90-degree angles (like we did in this living room), making sure there is no floor peeking through in between the rugs.

Layering rugs is a great solution if you have rugs that are stained in certain spots but you still love them.

BUDGET ANALYSIS

CONTRACTOR FEES	$2,692.00
WINDOW TREATMENTS	$758.70
LIGHTING	$2,133.18
FURNITURE	$1,668.95
FABRIC AND UPHOLSTERY	$1,988.00
BEDDING	$666.22
ART	$3,450.72
ACCESSORIES	$1,626.15
TOTAL	**$14,983.92**

Triplets' Bedroom

When Scott and Courtney Sternick asked us to come up with a few solutions for their triplets' bedroom, we jumped at the chance. We arrived at the Sternicks' two-bedroom apartment in New York City to find that their three-year-olds—two girls and a boy—were sharing a small, overcrowded room that had very little storage. The beds were lined up side by side, dormitory-style, taking up nearly all the floor space; what was left was blanketed in toys. Courtney had decorated in both hot pink and royal blue to make the space gender-neutral, but the color combination only added to the room's cramped, heavy feeling. There was barely any space to walk, let alone play, draw, read, or even sit down.

WHERE WE STARTED

THE BUDGET

$15,000

THE GOAL

To create three individual sleeping, work, and play spaces in a 12-by-15-foot bedroom

THE CLIENTS' WISH LIST

1. A new bedding system
2. Three individual work spaces
3. More storage
4. A unisex space
5. Overhead lighting

THE ALTERNATING COLORS MADE THE ROOM FEEL DARK, CLUTTERED, AND SLOPPY.

THIS WALL SPACE WASN'T BEING USED AT ALL.

HOPE I GET TO STAY!

The kids had way too many toys, most of which they didn't play with.

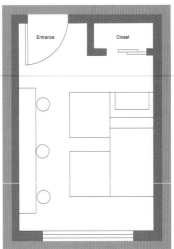

TIE-DYE IS NEVER A GOOD IDEA FOR HOME DECOR.

Our job was to come up with a solution to make the room more functional and less messy. Since we have seven children ourselves, this challenge was right up our alley. No matter where we've lived—be it a large town house or a small apartment—our children have shared bedrooms. We've always viewed at it as a positive—it's how they've learned to share and compromise. There was even a six-month stint when six of our kids lived in one tiny room in a temporary apartment. It was crowded but cozy, and they grew a whole lot closer. It also gave us great ideas for future projects and a love for the challenge of creating multifunctional spaces in small areas.

The upside of three kids sharing one room is that it makes life easier for the parents when kids aren't spread throughout a house or apartment, especially three three-year-olds. They can play together in their room, and one parent can be with all of the kids at the same time. However, there is still a need for some individual space. Our plan was to create a shared play space but to give each of the children their own work and sleep areas.

Our first task was to clear out the room. The kids had way too many toys, most of which they didn't play with. Like so many other parents, Scott and Courtney had a hard time downsizing the toy collection. But kids don't need tons of toys, and they get bored easily. We suggest getting rid of anything they haven't played with in the last two months.

DESIGN AND BUILD A NEW BEDDING SYSTEM

We wanted to give each child their own space while taking up as little room as possible. A custom-designed loft bed long enough to accommodate two twin beds below—with foot space in between—did the trick. It also meant we could keep two of the original beds as well as all three mattresses. The bottom beds contain storage space, and with the ladders on the sides of the loft bed, the kids feel like they have a jungle gym in their room.

The old hot pink and royal blue bedding and curtains were a nice attempt at making the room gender-neutral, but the combination made it feel small, dark, and messy. Instead, we chose a few vibrant colors and gave each bed its own unique look and identity.

SILK PILLOWS ADD TEXTURE, COLOR, AND FUN.

THE BED FRAME IS MADE OF KNOTTY-PINE-VENEER PLYWOOD.

THE PLATFORM WAS CONSTRUCTED WITH WHITE-LAMINATED PARTICLEBOARD.

THE DESK IS BIRCH-VENEER PLYWOOD WITH A CLEAR LACQUER FINISH.

THREE KIDS = THREE INDIVIDUAL WORK/ PLAY SPACES, WITH STORAGE, OF COURSE.

STEP 2

CREATE THREE INDIVIDUAL WORK SPACES

The kids love to play together, but they each needed their own workstation. With such limited space, the best solution was to custombuild one long desk with three partitions and three stools that tuck underneath. Each child got to pick which workstation was theirs, and each desk has its own storage space.

ASK THE EXPERT
TIM GEANY

Photographer Tim Geany gives us his tips on photographing kids:

- Always be on the lookout for special moments. Maybe the light is beautiful and the child is engaged in a natural activity and all you have to do is document the moment.
- Don't tell the kids to smile. Get them to smile, if you like. But remember, not all great photographs are of smiling subjects.
- It's always nice to get your kids to do something or play with friends or pets so they forget about the camera. Get them to engage.
- Keep your backgrounds simple.
- Learn to control your aperture to control your depth of focus.
- Dropping the background out of focus will simplify it.
- A faster shutter speed will stop action, and a slower shutter speed will blur action.
- Don't use a flash unless there is no other way to light the picture.
- Use a higher ISO.
- Create a style for your photographs so you have consistency when you show them off. It could be a special border, black-and-white, or desaturated color. There are a million effects to play with to come up with something great.

DECORATE THE WALLS

Instead of repainting the room, we decided to upgrade the light-blue wall with decals and create custom wallpaper. The colored dots, which are self-adhesive surface graphics (aka stickers) from Blik, come in sixteen colors and are quick and easy to install. Photographer Tim Geany had shot a series of photos of the kids with the intention of creating a photo collage above the desk. But when we saw the photos, both we and Scott and Courtney fell in love with one image above all others, and we used it to cover the entire wall.

WHAT KID DOESN'T LIKE DOTS?

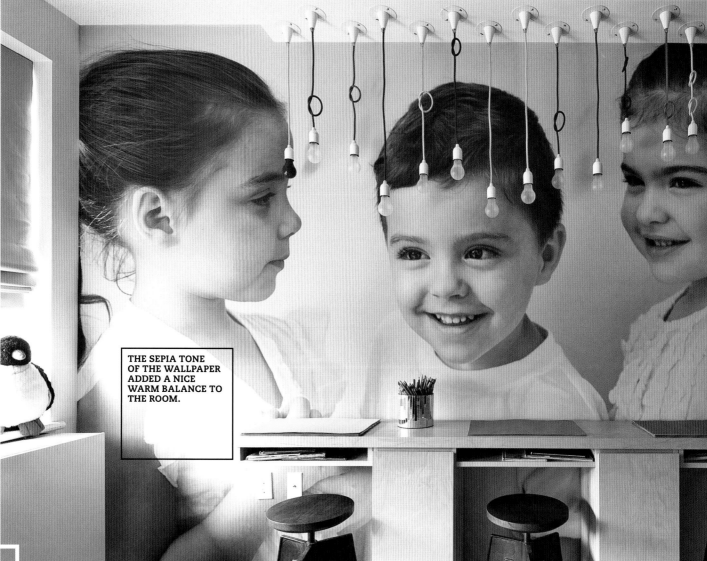

THE SEPIA TONE OF THE WALLPAPER ADDED A NICE WARM BALANCE TO THE ROOM.

THIS PIECE BY ARTIST KNOX MARTIN IS CHEERFUL AND COLORFUL, PERFECT FOR A KIDS' ROOM.

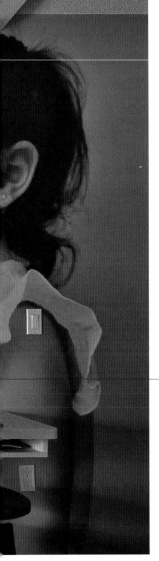

The colored dots come
in sixteen colors.

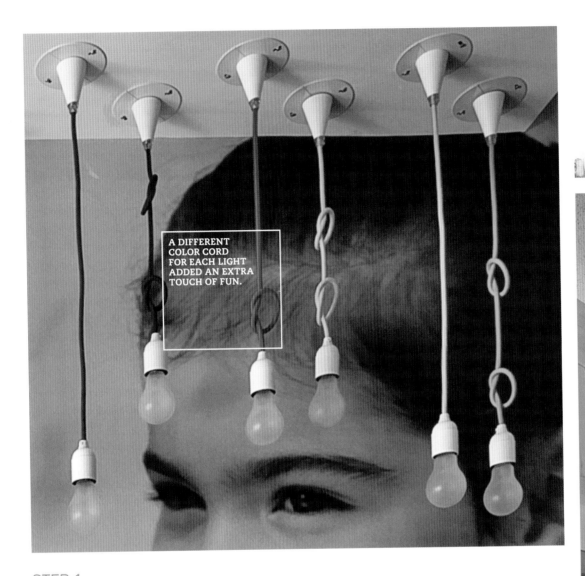

A DIFFERENT COLOR CORD FOR EACH LIGHT ADDED AN EXTRA TOUCH OF FUN.

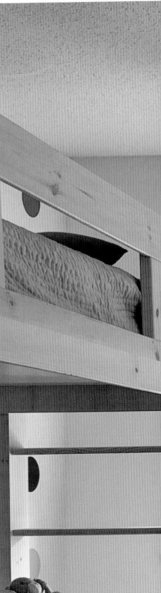

STEP 4

REDO THE LIGHTING

The room desperately needed overhead lighting, but because it was a rental, we couldn't break into the ceiling to add the electric. Our solution was to build a soffit that would conceal the wiring and hang the lights from there. The colorful NUD pendants give the kids plenty of light over their work area, and they light up the entire room. We tied loose knots into some of the cords, giving the pendants different lengths and adding to the playfulness of the space.

The colorful NUD pendants give the kids plenty of light over their work area.

AFTER: LIGHT, SIMPLE SHADE

THE PALE BLUE SHADE COMPLEMENTED THE PAINT AND DOTS, AND GAVE THE SPACE A MUCH CLEANER LOOK.

WHERE WE ENDED

The bedding and desk system transformed the space, allowing for extra play, work, and storage room while making everything look cleaner and more organized. In a small space, everything needs to be as streamlined as possible, but it can still be colorful and fun.

WE SAVED SOME MONEY BY KEEPING THE BLUE ON THIS WALL, THE THREE MATTRESSES, AND TWO OF THE BED FRAMES.

WE COULDN'T GET RID OF ALL THE TOYS. THERE'S STORAGE UNDERNEATH THESE BOTTOM TWO BEDS.

KEEP IT REAL!
WHEN SETTING UP
A PHOTO SHOOT,
HAVE KIDS DRESS
LIKE THEY DO
EVERY DAY . . . THAT
WAY THEY WILL
BE AS COMFORTABLE
AND HAPPY
AS POSSIBLE.

HOW TO

PLACE WALL STICKERS

CHOOSE A DESIGN

Be sure to pick a design that works for your space— in our case, dots— and remember it will be very large!

FIGURE OUT SPACING

Determine the distance between dots and the amount of wall space you plan to cover.

DRAW A GRID

We started at the top of the wall, 1 foot below the ceiling. We measured and made a small mark in pencil every 1 foot. Then we measured 1-foot lines up and down the wall and marked those as well.

APPLY THE STICKERS

Center a dot within each square of your grid. You can always peel it back up and recenter it.

CREATE WALLPAPER FROM A SINGLE IMAGE

MEASURE
Measure the area that you will be covering.

SELECT AN IMAGE
If you want to use an old photograph, it's best to scan the negative (instead of scanning the print). You will get the best resolution and a better-quality image. The image should be 150 dpi (dots per inch) at full size.

PLACE YOUR PAPER ORDER
Find a local or online printer that offers wallpaper printing. Give them the exact measurements of the wall or area of wall that you'd like to cover.

INSTALL AS YOU WOULD REGULAR WALLPAPER

BUDGET ANALYSIS

	CONTRACTOR FEES	$2,678.00
	PHOTO WALLPAPER	$2,017.00
	WALL DOTS	$270.00
	WINDOW TREATMENTS	$1,014.40
	LIGHTING	$832.65
	CUSTOM WOODWORK	$3,000.00
	STOOLS	$490.65
	BEDDING	$1,216.61
	PILLOWS	$500.20
	ART	GIFT
	TOTAL	**$12,019.51**

THE LOBBY:
IMPRESS WITH
YOUR BEST

Boutique Hotel

In 2008, developer and longtime client Dave Barry, with whom we'd worked on many projects, asked us to design a 25,000-square-foot, twenty-four-room boutique hotel in Long Branch, New Jersey, fifty-five miles south of New York City. We were ecstatic. This was our first commercial project and the most exciting one we'd ever been asked to do—it was literally the job we'd been dreaming of. It was also going to be the first luxury boutique hotel on the Jersey Shore.

When we drove down to the site, there was nothing but an empty lot. The hotel was going to be built from the ground up. Dave gave us free rein and full control of all the interiors, including the rooms, the lobby, and the bar. He asked that the place be chic but laid-back, with surfer art, wood, and a hip but warm lobby.

WHERE WE STARTED

THE BUDGET
$700,000

THE GOAL
To create a stylish twenty-four-room hotel with a chic, natural surfer vibe

THE CLIENT'S WISH LIST
1. Woodwork throughout
2. A great bar
3. A hip but comfortable lobby
4. A game area
5. White rooms with pops of color
6. Art everywhere

IN PROGRESS

ALMOS
THERE

THE BAR/LOUNGE/ GAME AREA GETS GREAT LIGHT.

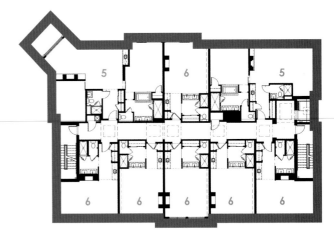

Our plan was to create a lounge and a bar area that were comfortable yet stylish, with great art and sophisticated but fun design. We also planned to bring the outside in as much as possible by using natural elements throughout. We wanted guests to feel transformed as soon as they walked in the door. The goal was to create something that no one had seen before.

We worked with the architect, Glenn Haydu of Minno and Wasko, from the very beginning. Together, we were able to decide details that would influence the design. Everything—from where the bathtubs would be installed to where each electrical outlet would be placed—was an important decision. Being involved in the process from such an early stage made the whole process much smoother and each of our ideas more doable.

SURFER ART, SETTING THE MOOD FROM THE MOMENT YOU CHECK IN

THE QUEEN BY ANN CARRINGTON

STEP 1
DESIGN THE LOBBY

Our task with the lobby and lounge area was to create a chic, laid-back surfer vibe. We aimed to make it inviting and warm, a place to feel like you can kick your shoes off as soon as you walk in, yet without forgoing style. But it also had to be durable—commercial spaces need to be far more resilient than residential ones.

Craftsman John Houshmand executed our vision for the wood-work for the bar, lobby, and game area flawlessly. We literally brought the outdoors in, using finished, polished pieces in some areas (the stools, the columns, the bar), and more rustic pieces in other areas (the birch tree trunks). The idea behind all of the wood was to use it to soften and warm up the whole space.

The three sofas came from eBay, and although none of them was in great shape when we bought them, each one had huge potential. We had them reupholstered with different fabrics—one in leather, the second in faux ostrich, and the third in faux cowhide. The faux ostrich sofa had upholstery nails that we removed and replaced with large gunmetal nails, and we lacquered the wood in black. The frame of the black leather sofa was painted a glossy white for contrast. The oversized cocktail tables were custom made in Peru. The light-colored wood is reminiscent of the seaside and is a great balance to the dark vintage sofas.

SHEERS ADD ELEGANCE AND LET THE LIGHT SHINE THROUGH.

REUPHOLSTERED IN BLACK LEATHER

We aimed to make the lobby inviting and warm.

ASK THE EXPERT
GLENN HAYDU

We asked architect Glenn Haydu, of Minno and Wasko, for his thoughts on building the hotel.

Q: Tell us about the project.

A: The exterior is modern, with metallic and wood elements, and the interior is clean, simple, and comfortable for kids and adults. Anyone who comes to this hotel is going to remember multiple design aspects that they do not find at other properties.

Q: What were the challenges?

A: The site is the gateway to Pier Village, so it required a memorable design. And due to the location and prominence, many people were involved—the local officials, the owner, the general contractor, and, of course, the design team. That makes it challenging to satisfy everyone's wants and desires within a budget.

Q: What is the best scenario for designers and architects working together?

A: Meeting early and often. Too many projects do not include all of the design participants early enough, which can lead to restrictions in the design process or late, costly changes, impacting time and budgets. And flexibility. No one can get their way on every aspect of the project, so the team must make certain concessions continually throughout the process, collaborating and blending the expertise of each participant.

TOM DIXON LIGHTS

AN ANTIQUE DARTBOARD MAKES FOR GREAT ART.

GREAT DISPLAY SPACE

STEP 2

DESIGN THE BAR

With the help of talented craftsman John Houshmand, we were able to create a totally unique storage solution and bar/lounge atmosphere. The shelves behind the bar store the alcohol, while the shelves next to the bar are filled with art, design, and travel books; small pieces we picked up at flea markets and vintage stores; and old jars and bottles, some filled with sand.

The three chrome lights that hang above the bar are Tom Dixon pendants. At night, they make the bar feel sleek and cool; during the day, they make it feel fun and playful.

The wood bar stools (as well as the stools throughout the lobby) were custom made.

GAMES TO
ENTERTAIN
ANY AGE

DESIGN THE GAME AREA

We wanted the game area to be cool enough to hang out in on a Saturday night but also fun for kids to spend time in during a break from the sun or on a rainy day. The vintage pool table, a Brunswick from the 1940s, is the room's focal point. The feather light that hangs above the table brightens it up. Artist Heidi Cody designed the "Bungalow" light boxes, with each letter from an old-school logo.

The birch trees serve as a divider for the rest of the space without cutting it off or closing it in. The two garage doors are great for connecting the interior space to the patio. On sunny days, when the garage doors are open, the lounge suddenly becomes a large, outdoor space.

WE LOVE
BRINGING THE
OUTSIDE IN.

The birch trees serve as a divider
for the rest of the space.

PICK THE ART

The walls in the bar, lobby, and most of the rooms are wide and the ceilings are high, so we painted everything white to make the hotel feel like an art gallery. We brought in more than fifty original works of art and hung them throughout the hotel. Much of the art is surfing- and beach-inspired, including works by Patrick Cariou, Jeff Devine, and Tony Caramanico, which gives the space an old-school beach town feel. *The Queen*, which hangs above the lounge area, is a piece by Ann Carrington.

THIS WAS CREATED ENTIRELY OUT OF BUTTONS.

Much of the art is surfing- and beach-inspired.

OCEAN-BLUE WALLPAPER

THE TULIP BRINGS THE HALLWAY TO LIFE.

KENNY SCHACHTER

We asked our friend and favorite art dealer, Kenny Schachter, a few questions on art and the art world.

Q: How do you suggest someone start collecting?

A: The best way to get started is to go slow—do due diligence; there is no harm in waiting. Contemporary art gets made and made and made. It's not going anywhere. On the other hand, if you are impulsive like me and from time to time need to make a jump for something, then start small. A lot can be done with the discipline of a self-imposed tight budget, say from $500 to $1,500 or thereabouts.

Q: Where do you find works by young and emerging artists?

A: You find accessible art at the degree shows of art schools, and whenever there is a big commercial art fair, there are normally a few million (it tends to feel like that) ancillary fairs that offer up works by emerging artists at a lower cost.

Q: Should you buy what you like or what you think is a good investment?

A: Only buy what you love, but there is no reason that can't correspond with what is a good investment if you buy wisely and with prudence.

Q: What are your thoughts on art fairs?

A: I absolutely adore art fairs, as long as I don't have to be in them and suffer the juvenile, capricious politics that engulf them all. Unlike at auctions, you can still see some of the very best art, but there is no public record of any transactions. When you buy at the auction houses Sotheby's, Christie's, or Phillips, that information has a shelf life longer than that of carbon, appearing in auction databases until the end of time, whereas at fairs, you only contend with the short memories of most fairgoers.

ANN CARRINGTON

Artist Ann Carrington, who is a good friend of ours, created flags from twenty-four coastal countries, one for each of the rooms. We asked her a few questions about the flags, her art, and her story.

Q: Tell us about the U.S. flag.

A: Denim always evokes the Wild West and cowboys. I think of this piece [*Stars and Stripes*] as a giant drawing—but the drawing is done in denim. I collected hundreds of pairs of very old, faded jeans for the lighter stripes on the flag, and hundreds of pairs of newer jeans for the darker stripes. I then cut the waistbands off to make the stripes and pieced them together with my industrial sewing machine. The stars were made by making a little hole in the denim and then fraying the denim into a star shape.

Q: Where do you get your inspiration?

A: I keep sketchbooks and diaries, which are visual documentations of my ideas for artworks. In them you will find everything—fruit wrappers, stamps, postcards, lottery tickets—a paper world where football stickers, Brazilian coffee labels, and local bus tickets rub shoulders with images of pop stars and dancing girls from the Congo! I take inspiration from many diverse sources: pop culture, museums, poetry, folk art, scrap yards, foreign cultures.

Q: Why found objects?

A: Using found materials, for me, is about observation, lateral thinking, and an awareness of everything in the world. There is a great wealth of resources waiting to be used, from virgin materials to others that have been exploited or discarded, and I approach them all indiscriminately. The resulting artworks comment indirectly on the throwaway culture that has nourished them and also on the artistic climate that helped pave their way—a route laid down by the likes of Picasso and Braque, whose African-inspired constructions suggested that modeling clay and chiseling stone were not the only material options for a sculptor. I like my artworks to tell a story, and the materials are part and parcel of that.

Q: Is there anything you won't work with?

A: Everything in the world has the potential to be an artwork; it's all about lateral thinking and taking a sideways look at a familiar (or not familiar) object—seeing it in a new context and then making it into art!

Q: Why should people have art in their homes?

A: I think there is a natural instinct in us all to want to surround ourselves with images in our homes, whether it be posters, fine art, family photographs, sculptures, our children's artwork. I am always amazed when I look at Neolithic cave drawings of bison and mammoths—it was the same impulse.

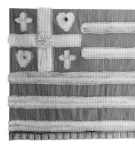

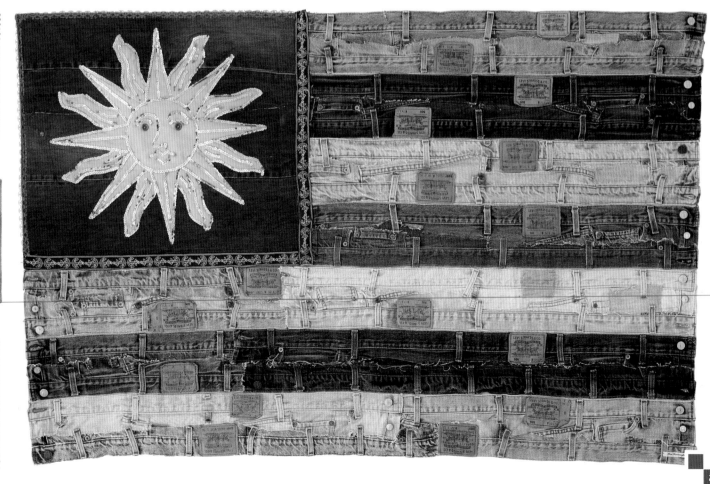

DESIGN THE ROOMS

Our goal here was to create large, clean-lined, open rooms that would all have their own unique details. The furniture, bathroom fixtures, bedding, and other basics are uniform throughout the hotel, but each room has its own throw pillows, blankets, artwork, and accessories.

Because durability was so important, we laid high-gloss white engineered wood floors that could withstand heavy traffic. The white is a great canvas for the furniture, art, and rugs. The bedding and linens throughout are white, too. It's the rugs, pillows, vintage blankets, and artwork that bring in all the color and texture.

THE MODERN WHITE SOFAS FROM KARTELL ARE BOTH SIMPLE AND LAID-BACK.

CUSTOM BEDS AND BUILT-IN SIDE TABLES ALLOW FOR EASY MAINTENANCE.

THE COTTON DRAPES ARE SOFT AND FLOWING, WHILE THE SHEERS ALLOW NATURAL LIGHT TO POUR IN.

THE GAS FIREPLACES MAKE EVERYTHING WARMER ON CHILLY NIGHTS.

THE DINING TABLES WERE CUSTOM MADE; THE BLACK DINING CHAIRS ARE ALSO FROM KARTELL.

CHANDELIER ABOVE THE TUB = ROMANTIC (JUST USE CANDLES, NOT ELECTRICITY)

SURF REPORT
FOR JUNE 8, 2009
AIR TEMP: 84°F
H₂O TEMP: 68°F
WAVES: PERFECT

THE BULLETIN BOARD AND CHALKBOARD ADD A SENSE OF HUMOR AND PLAYFULNESS.

THE COWHIDE RUGS ADD COLOR AND TEXTURE.

STEP 6

DESIGN AND INSTALL THE BATHROOMS

There are four different layouts for the rooms and for the bathrooms. In some of the larger suites, we chose to install bathtubs that were open to the room. This turned out to be one of our favorite design elements, although it's not for the shy! We hung black candelabras above the tubs for some added romance.

Each room has twin sinks and cubicles for the toilet and shower—clean and modern. Inexpensive white tile was used throughout, but high-end hardware adds sophistication and is an important detail.

Floating mirrors above the sinks that have chalkboards and corkboards on the flip side are fun, quirky, and playful.

EACH ROOM FEATURES THE FLAG OF A DIFFERENT COASTAL COUNTRY, ALL HANDMADE BY ARTIST ANN CARRINGTON.

WHITE BRINGS A SENSE OF CALM TO ANY SPACE.

WHERE WE ENDED

The natural elements provide a laid-back surfer vibe, while the furnishings and art bring a chic, sophisticated look to the Jersey Shore.

WE
DESIGNED
THE BOY/
GIRL RUG.

TURN A FLEA-MARKET FIND INTO A STUNNING PIECE OF FURNITURE

We have found some of our favorite pieces at flea markets, estate sales, and vintage stores, and on eBay and Etsy. (If purchasing online, ask plenty of questions about the condition of the item before you make the purchase.)

INSPECT THE PIECE.
Make sure that the piece has good bones and shape, since everything else about it (the fabric, the color) is going to change.

CHOOSE AN UPHOLSTERER.
Find a good upholsterer in your area. It's always a good idea to call around and get a few cost estimates. Send them a photo ahead of time so they can tell you how much fabric you'll need.

PICK YOUR FABRIC.
You can shop for fabric online, but seeing it and touching it in person is always best. Look for a durable fabric, and of course pick a pattern, print, or solid that works with the piece you've chosen as well as with the overall decor of the space. If you stick with a solid color, have fun with texture to give the piece some depth. And don't forget to consider adding or changing the piping.

ACCESSORIZE!
Get creative. You can add or change the buttons and/or the tufting. This can completely change the look and feel of a chair or sofa.

SELECT THE PAINT.
If the wood on the chair or sofa is in bad condition, or if you want to modernize the piece, have the wood painted. Most upholsterers will be able to do this for you. We like to use high-gloss paint for a modern feel. If you want something to look more aged, many places can do a "distressed" look.

BUDGET ANALYSIS

WINDOW TREATMENTS	$75,000.00
CUSTOM WOODWORKING	$200,000.00
LOBBY	$17,900.00
BAR	$19,760.00
LOUNGE	$45,100.00
GAME AREA	$49,800.00
STANDARD BEDROOMS (16)	$131,472.00
SUITES (8)	$126,856.00
OUTDOOR PATIO	$20,939.00
MISCELLANEOUS	$31,400.00
TOTAL	$718,227.00

COOL

Beach House

Shortly after the birth of our seventh child, a couple came to us and asked if we could renovate a place they owned in the Hamptons. They had an old, run-down house on their property that they hoped could be transformed into a proper guesthouse. We were a little hesitant to take an out-of-town job with a new baby, but when we saw what the project entailed—knocking down tons of walls and redoing all the interiors—we couldn't refuse. Gut jobs are our hands-down favorites. So we made it work: one of us drove the two or three hours to work on the guesthouse while the other stayed in Manhattan with the kids.

The owners needed the place completed by Memorial Day, when the first of their summer guests would arrive. This meant we had less than two months to finish the project.

WHERE WE STARTED

THE BUDGET

$300,000

THE GOAL

To turn an old, run-down house into a modernized, relaxed beach house

THE CLIENTS' WISH LIST

1. An open floor plan
2. Fresh paint throughout
3. Renovated bathrooms
4. A new kitchen

THE WALLS WERE UNEVEN AND POORLY CONSTRUCTED.

THE FLOORS THROUGHOUT WERE WARPED AND DAMAGED.

The place was dark and musty.

2ND FLOOR

MAIN FLOOR

BASEMENT

BROWN
AND BLAH

The large five-bedroom, four-bathroom house hadn't been updated since the 1970s. The place was dark and musty, the rooms were cramped, and the creaky floors made it feel creepy. The grounds, like many in the Hamptons, were spectacular. But inside the house, there was no sense that it was situated on one of the most beautiful places on earth. The inside needed to be gutted.

Our first task was to tear down almost every interior wall on the main floor. The existing main-floor living area consisted of four small, boxed-in rooms: kitchen, living room, dining room, and den. (There were also two bedrooms and a bathroom on the other side of the house, but we left them where they were.) We moved the kitchen from the center to the front of the house so that it would be open to the living and dining areas.

The original bathrooms had been tiled in pale colors, with tubs and toilets to match—which might have looked stylish back in the day but forty years later looked dirty, dated, and cheap. Tiles, tubs, sinks, and toilets were all ripped out.

When we were done, all that was left were the hardwood floors.

STEP 1

REDO THE FLOORS AND WALLS

Because so much of the budget was earmarked for construction, we had to be especially careful with the design of the rest of the house. We decided not to install new hardwood floors, but the existing floors were in such bad condition that something had to be done. Repairing them in places, sanding them down, and painting them white transformed the entire place. The effect was so strong that we just kept on painting. Everything went white—the walls, the staircases, the basement, and the second-level floors.

REDO THE KITCHEN

The goal was an open white kitchen with a few key pops of color. The countertops and cabinets were both purchased at Ikea and are sleek, modern, and inexpensive. We found the black chandeliers at Home Depot while purchasing building supplies. They were incredibly inexpensive, but you would never know—and they add a hip elegance to the kitchen.

THE YELLOW AND WHITE COUNTERTOP IS FROM IKEA AND IS THREE SLABS SANDWICHED ON TOP OF EACH OTHER, MAKING IT EXTRA THICK.

THE YELLOW STOVE IS FROM BLUESTAR.

The goal was an open white kitchen with a few pops of color.

FAUX
HIDES ARE
FUN AND
INEXPENSIVE.

FURNISH THE LIVING AND DINING AREAS

The clients had storage units filled with furniture, art, and rugs from many previous homes. We knew the clients had good taste, but we didn't know if we would find red couches, blue rugs, or striped chairs. Turns out almost all the furniture was white. Given how white the rest of the house was, we needed to add pops of color to the couches, chairs, and tables. Pillows, art, and small accessories brought the furnishings to life and made the space feel like a home. French doors were installed in place of the sliding glass doors that led from the living and dining areas out to the deck.

FRENCH
DOORS ARE
CLASSIC
AND
ELEGANT.

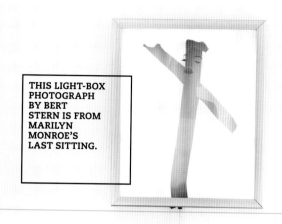

THIS LIGHT-BOX
PHOTOGRAPH
BY BERT
STERN IS FROM
MARILYN
MONROE'S
LAST SITTING.

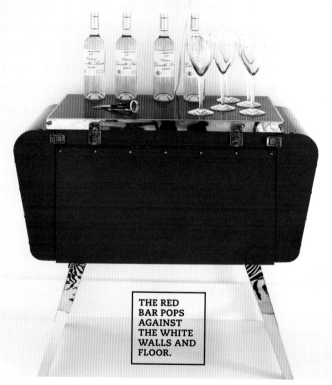

THE RED
BAR POPS
AGAINST
THE WHITE
WALLS AND
FLOOR.

STEVEN SACKS

We asked Steven Sacks, the director and owner of Bitforms Gallery, for his thoughts on media art.

Q: Is media art a fad or a staple?

A: Let's start by defining *new media art*, a term that is challenging and not always accurate. New media as a concept or a genre is based on tapping into the most contemporary tools and ideas of a specific time period and applying these innovative methods to the artist's practice. Many of these methods include time-based media. Media art is an integral part of the art world and should be a part of any contemporary art collection.

Q: What do you love about it?

A: The reason I focused on new media art was to witness innovation develop in the art world. I love a great traditional painting, sculpture, or drawing, but there is enough of that being represented. I react to the unexpected interpretations that media tools can afford the artist.

Q: How has media art evolved?

A: Since I opened my gallery in 2001, new media, which is typically more experimental and can be more challenging to collect, has seen a rise in acceptance and exposure in the art world. The quality of the work has improved, and there is a larger range of artists who are participating.

Q: Where can you see it? Where can you purchase it?

A: As with all types of art, you can find media works in many art galleries around the world. New York City's Chelsea area probably has the most offerings. Many gallery websites have video clips showing documentation of works that are time-based or are active sculptures. It's best to see the work in person if possible, but many sales take place online. Galleries that tend to focus on media art, like mine does, will have more experience with installation options and maintenance issues.

Q: What's your favorite piece and why?

A: As a gallerist, I don't have a favorite piece of art. My attraction is the range of media and ideas that are constantly streaming through my gallery. Each day I discover a new favorite.

REBUILD THE STAIRCASES

The staircases were in bad shape and didn't fit well in the space. We reconfigured the layout and had them rebuilt, installing simple railings and painting everything white. The stair risers were painted black, and the stenciling was layered on top.

ASK THE EXPERT
NORMA KAMALI

We asked fashion designer Norma Kamali a few questions about creativity, design, and where she gets her inspiration.

Q: Do you believe it's more important to be timeless or current?

A: Both. It is very important to design the antiques of the future, the styles people will want long after they were developed. There is never the outright intention to do that, but a subliminal thought like that would be a great advantage.

Q: Your store is very white. What's your theory on incorporating color?

A: People are color, and so are the clothing and paper mannequins we display. The clean environment is like a blank canvas that transforms with new displays and collections.

Q: Does fashion have an influence on interiors and/or vice versa?

A: I think personal style carries to the home and people tend to want to live in an environment that reflects how they dress or at least the aesthetic they feel comfortable in.

Q: Where do you get your inspiration from?

A: Everywhere, every day. But especially when I think about the future, about doing what hasn't been done before.

Q: What are you inspired by when you leave the city?

A: I think leaving the city or going to the gym or having a good conversation can take you away from what you do daily and give your mind a chance to let waiting ideas become real thoughts and concepts you can make into something. The beauty of being creative is that it is part of your DNA. It can happen at any moment. It doesn't need to be controlled. Like breathing.

BEFORE

ONE INTERESTING PIECE ADDS CHARACTER.

THE ARTWORK BROUGHT IN A TON OF COLOR.

OFTENTIMES, THE EASIEST REMEDY IS PAINT.

STEP 5

REDO THE MASTER BEDROOM AND THE BATHROOMS

The existing master bedroom had brown wall-to-wall carpeting, sliding doors to the balcony, and a dated en suite bathroom. Once the furniture was gone and the carpeting had been ripped out, everything was painted white. Elegant French doors replaced the sliders and simple white drapes were hung over the doors.

The furniture came from the clients' storage units, but the black king-sized platform bed felt too plain in the large white space. Splattering pink, white, and blue paint all over the headboard added much-needed texture, color, and fun to the room.

All four bathrooms had forty-year-old pastel-colored tile, tubs, sinks, and toilets. The white subway tiles made everything sleek and new without breaking the bank. White tubs, toilets, and sinks followed.

GAMES

THIS IS OUR FAVORITE PIECE.

REDO THE GAME ROOM

Because the house was built into a hill, the large basement opened to the outside from the back. We painted the floors and walls white, as we did in the rest of the house. A second seating area, perfect for the TV, was created, as well as a large game room. The new mini-bar, which includes a refrigerator and a draught-beer dispenser, allows pool games to continue without interruption from trips to get drinks from upstairs. The focal point of the basement is the 1942 Brunswick pool table. The bright orange top totally pops against the stark white floors and walls.

The focal point of the basement is the 1942 Brunswick pool table.

ASK THE EXPERT
HARRY GROZIO

Harry Grozio, owner of Grozio's Antiques, is an expert when it comes to locating, restoring, and refinishing antique pool tables. We've purchased a few vintage tables from him over the years. He knows pool tables better than maybe anyone, and he gives everyone a good price.

Q: Why are pool tables an asset to the home?
A: Because they end up being a focal point in most homes—a place for entertainment, gatherings, and spending time with friends and family.

Q: Vintage or new?
A: Vintage tables hold their value. You can get quality new tables, but they are more expensive and the wood isn't of as great a quality as that of the old ones. A new table is like a new car—it loses value as soon as it leaves the shop.

Q: What are some secrets to finding vintage tables?
A: I've been hanging around hustlers, players, and billiard rooms for fifty years, and I pay finder's fees. I have a lot of eyes out in the field looking for me.

Q: What size room do you recommend for a pool table?
A: There needs to be 5 feet around the sides of the table. The smallest table is 3 feet by 6 feet, so the room would need to be at least 13 by 16. Regulation tables are 5 feet by 10 feet, so the room needs to be at least 15 by 20.

Q: Ping-Pong or pool?
A: Funny . . . actually, I have built a number of Ping-Pong tops to go over pool tables— it works nicely.

INSTALL LIGHT BOXES

We often see something that we love and then look for ways to achieve the same look or idea within a budget, which is what we did with the light boxes outside the front door. A graphic designer friend of ours drew the maps of Long Island, and our carpenter, Tom Baione, built the wood boxes and installed the lighting and wiring within them. They bring much-needed light to the front door and are a fun and unique alternative to a traditional sconce. They have a beachy look that sets the mood for what awaits on the other side.

MAKING THE LIGHT BOXES OURSELVES COST A QUARTER OF WHAT IT WOULD HAVE TO BUY THEM.

The light boxes bring much-needed light to the front door.

WHERE WE ENDED

Most of the interior walls were torn down, and the walls, ceilings, and floors were all painted white, making the space feel four times larger.

THE WHITE FLOORS UNIFY THE SPACE.

OUTDOOR
TABLES
CAN WORK
INSIDE.

TIPS AND TRICKS

TIPS ON PAINTING FLOORS WHITE

1. Before you begin, vacuum and wipe down the floors, removing all dust and dirt.

2. Use a polyurethane-based porch and floor enamel.

3. Paint the edges with a brush, then use a roller to paint the rest.

4. Keep the first coat of paint thin.

5. Add two more thin layers, allowing twenty-four hours between each coat.

THE PROS AND CONS OF WHITE WOOD FLOORS

PROS

They make any space seem much larger.

They give a space an open, loftlike feel.

They showcase the furniture, making it pop.

They brighten up any space.

Almost anything looks good on white.

CONS

They get dirty quickly and easily.

BUDGET ANALYSIS

	CONTRACTOR FEES	$260,000.00
	WINDOW TREATMENTS	$5,200.00
	LIGHTING	$325.00
	KITCHEN REMODEL	$4,600.00
	APPLIANCES	$8,200.00
	BATHROOM REMODELS	$6,750.00
	MINIBAR	$770.00
	BAR CART	$600.00
	POOL TABLE	$10,000.00
	LIGHT BOXES	$750.00
	ACCESSORIES	$500.00
	TOTAL	**$297,695.00**

ANNA

Brooklyn Modern

We met Anna Skiba-Crafts and Benjamin Nathan (and their cat, Billy) a couple of years after they purchased their first home in the up-and-coming neighborhood of Red Hook, Brooklyn. Their home is a modern duplex with tons of windows, situated between two old brick town houses. It has an open first floor and a bedroom upstairs with a private terrace. Though they'd been living there for two years when we arrived, they hadn't quite figured out how to best utilize their space, nor had they decorated it. Similar to other clients we have encountered, they weren't really sure where to start, so they never did.

WHERE WE STARTED

THE BUDGET

$40,000

THE GOAL

To create a multifunctional first level that would also be suitable for entertaining and to craft a cozy-but-chic bedroom upstairs.

THE CLIENTS' WISH LIST

1. A dining table for four to six
2. Comfortable furniture
3. An office area for two
4. Additional storage space
5. Better use of the nook at the top of the stairs
6. Privacy (particularly upstairs)

THE LIVING ROOM LACKED COLOR.

Anna and Ben both wanted an industrial look with traditional touches.

CRAMPED BEDROOM WITH TOO MUCH FURNITURE

While Anna and Ben had been living in a white box, they wanted color but just hadn't been able to pull the trigger themselves. The first floor needed to serve multiple functions, but the layout didn't allow for that. There was no real flow, and the space had to be reworked so that it could be better used for entertaining.

The apartment is fairly wide, with a good footprint to work with, though the two levels combined equal only 900 square feet. There are angles throughout that create great lines, but also some odd pockets of space. We knew we would have to get creative and utilize everything available to us.

Anna and Ben both wanted an industrial look with traditional touches. And, like us, they love a mix of antique and modern. Our goal was to create a colorful, comfortable home with a few whimsical touches.

INEFFICIENT WORK SPACE

THE SMALLER BOOKS WENT ON THE SHELVES WHILE THE LARGER ONES WERE PLACED ON EITHER SIDE OF THE CHEST.

STEP 1

DESIGN THE LIVING AREA

Anna and Ben weren't attached to any of their existing furniture, so we got rid of everything except their mattress. Once the space was emptied out, we repainted the main level a very pale blue. Ben and Anna wanted color, but because the first floor flows seamlessly into the second floor, we needed to keep the walls a uniform shade. Pale blue was as drastic as we felt we could go without overpowering the upstairs.

Anna and Ben's furnishings didn't allow for much flexibility, so finding pieces that were more versatile and better scaled to the size of the room was key. We replaced their bulky couch with a tailored one and their large glass coffee table with two ottomans. We also softened the very contemporary space by using a traditional antique credenza that stores twice as much as the media cabinet it replaced.

MEDIA CABINETS CAN BE GORGEOUS

THESE OTTOMAN TABLES CAN BE CONVERTED INTO EXTRA SEATING.

NO MORE EATING MEALS OFF THE COFFEE TABLE

CREATE A DINING AREA

Anna and Ben were eager to entertain, but they didn't know how to fit a dining table and chairs into the living area. We combined the two office spaces that had been at opposite sides of the room into one shared space underneath the stairs, thereby making room for a proper dining area.

The antique farm table came from Greenhouse, a vintage store in Brooklyn, and adds warmth to the space. The seat of each vintage metal chair was covered with different fabric, for a quirky touch. Anchored by the chandelier, this area is a balance of old and new. The piece behind the table is a photograph of Ben and Anna taken by photographer Catherine Hall. Our carpenter, Tom Baione, did a fantastic job covering the beam and columns with wood detailing.

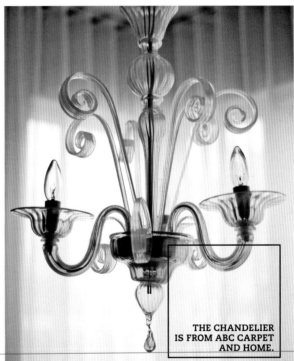

THE CHANDELIER IS FROM ABC CARPET AND HOME.

Finding pieces that were versatile was key.

THESE LIGHTS BRING IN TEXTURE AND CHARACTER

THREE COUNTER STOOLS ARE BETTER THAN TWO.

STEP 3

BRING LIFE TO THE KITCHEN

The kitchen was in excellent shape but needed some major flair. The glass lamps hanging above the island were too small and got lost, so we replaced them with industrial perforated cage lights, which add a great rustic touch. We also replaced Anna and Ben's white plastic bar stools with three simple stools that are a better contrast against the white kitchen island.

ABOVE THE CABINETS, ROOM FOR THE COOKBOOKS

RETHINK THE OFFICE SPACE

The area underneath the stairs had been used for storage and one of the two office spaces, but it was awkward and felt messy and cluttered. We started with a great industrial table that would allow for more depth than a desk and space for two to work side by side. We purchased the vintage chairs, designed by Ray Komai, at Bright Lyons in Brooklyn. The pink file cabinet is a great solution for all of Anna and Ben's papers and clutter.

THE DESK IS AN INDUSTRIAL TABLE THAT CAME FROM CRAIGSLIST.

THIS PINK FILE CABINET IS A GREAT POP OF COLOR— IT FITS THE SPACE PERFECTLY, TOO.

THE VINTAGE CHAIRS CAN ALSO DOUBLE AS EXTRA SEATING FOR DINNER GUESTS.

We started with a great industrial table.

REDO THE STAIRCASE AND LANDING NOOK

The staircase is gorgeous, but the area surrounding it was in need of some life. The tonal blue-and-white Vistosi light fixture over the stairway was perfectly framed by the vertical windows and can be enjoyed from inside or out.

The nook at the top of the stairs was probably our biggest challenge. It had been filled with books, but the bookshelves weren't very accessible, because the space tapers as you move into it. We emptied it out and brought the books downstairs. Since using this space for storage wasn't an option in terms of efficiency, we decided to build a custom seating area to create another place to enjoy. The pillows and the pouf add texture and turn the space into a cozy escape.

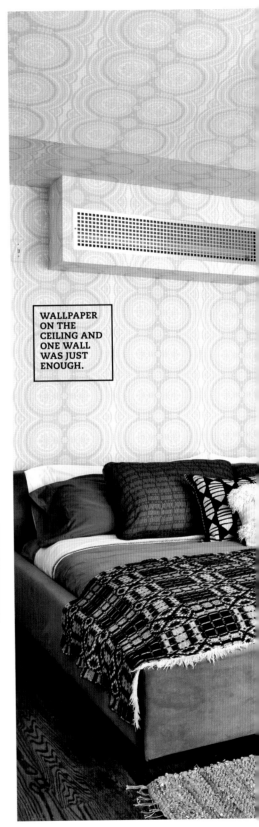

WALLPAPER ON THE CEILING AND ONE WALL WAS JUST ENOUGH.

A PLACE WITH TOYS FOR BILLY

STEP 6

REDESIGN THE BEDROOM

Our main task with the bedroom was to declutter and streamline the space. There was too much furniture, including an oversized Eames chair that blocked access to the terrace. We removed everything aside from the mattress, and started from scratch. The AC unit over the bed was an eyesore, so Tom built a box for it, and when we wallpapered the ceiling and the wall behind the bed, we camouflaged and wrapped it as well. The wallpaper warms up the room and makes it feel special.

The bed is from CB2. It's simple, but the plush gray color adds a soft elegance. The bedding was replaced with a colorful collection of high-end sheets, pillows, and shams, along with a blue-and-white vintage throw.

The two sets of doors leading to the terrace let in lots of light, so we installed sheers on a track so they could easily be opened or closed for privacy.

WHERE WE ENDED

Replacing the furniture with items that better fit the space and could be moved around for entertaining was an important piece of the puzzle in making Anna and Ben's home more functional. We combined two separate office areas to make room for a dining space, and through the use of color and texture, we transformed the bedroom into a private oasis.

BOOKS CAN BE
A GREAT DESIGN
ELEMENT.

INCORPORATE
WOOD IN A
CONTEMPORARY
SPACE TO
WARM IT UP.

THE RUG HELPS
TO DEFINE THE
SEATING AREA AND
BRINGS IN MUCH-
NEEDED COLOR.

HOW TO

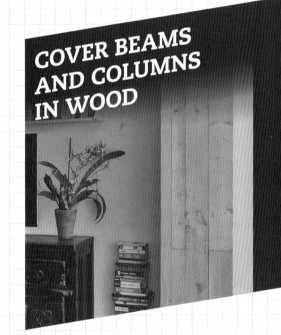

COVER BEAMS AND COLUMNS IN WOOD

TAKE MEASUREMENTS
Measure the beams or columns to find out how much coverage will be needed.

PURCHASE THE WOOD
We used unpainted picket fencing from Home Depot because the boards were essentially precut (we just needed to remove the top points).

ATTACH THE PLANKS
Nail the boards to the columns and beams.

PAINT THE BOARDS
We diluted the paint with water and used a rag to rub it onto the wood. It left a bit of the natural grain showing but toned down the yellow hue of that particular wood.

BUDGET ANALYSIS

CONTRACTOR FEES	$4,500.00
WALLPAPER AND INSTALLATION	$3,917.85
PAINT	$520.35
WINDOW TREATMENTS	$1,862.42
LIGHTING AND REWIRING	$6,875.18
CUSTOM WOODWORKING	$1,450.00
FURNITURE	$10,853.21
RUGS	$875.35
BEDDING	$1,201.92
ART	$2,209.37
ACCESSORIES	$4,646.68
CAT TOYS AND ACCESSORIES	$322.09
TOTAL	$39,234.42

THIS LAMP BASE IS MADE OF LEGO PIECES!

Last-Minute Nursery

We met Karl and Melanie Haller when she was within a few weeks of giving birth to their second son. They needed a nursery and were running out of time. They'd moved into their three-bedroom, three-bathroom apartment on the Upper West Side of Manhattan six months before and hadn't quite finished unpacking. Between caring for their three-year-old son, Griffin, and juggling two busy careers in the fashion industry, they hadn't had much time to design, decorate, or shop for the new apartment.

Their place is in a classic prewar building and has beautiful hardwood floors and gorgeous moldings, baseboards, and detailing throughout. It had been recently renovated and was in pristine condition. The problem was that the decor did not match the

WHERE WE STARTED

THE BUDGET

$20,000

THE GOAL

To create a temporary nursery that would eventually transition to a guest room, and to design a stylish and functional kid's room

THE CLIENTS' WISH LIST

1. A crib and a changing table
2. A convertible sofa bed
3. New lighting
4. Wallpaper
5. Paint
6. Kid-friendly but modern and stylish touches

PRISTINE CONDITION BUT NO SOUL

The decor did not match the quality of the apartment.

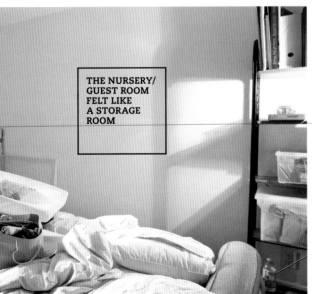

THE NURSERY/
GUEST ROOM
FELT LIKE
A STORAGE
ROOM

quality of the apartment—Karl and Melanie had set up shop with the bare essentials, with plans to do more as soon as they had time. We often see clients become paralyzed after purchasing a new home—especially when the home is as nice as the Hallers'. It's easy to end up doing very little for fear of making the wrong design choices. And between their hectic schedules and their indecisiveness, the Hallers were in need of some assistance.

The room set aside for the nursery was full of unpacked boxes and storage items. The plan was to create a space that could also be used for guests and eventually become a full-time guest room. And while we were at it, they asked if we could also give Griffin's room an upgrade. It had the basics but needed color, light, and a few creative design solutions.

The two rooms are similar in that they both are rectangular but spacious, with high ceilings and large windows at the far end. Both get nice light during the daytime, but neither had much lighting, overhead or otherwise, which was an issue at night. Installing overhead lighting wasn't in the budget, so we had to get creative with fun and functional lamps. Since the nursery was going to double as a guest room for now, we also had to figure out how to make it multifunctional without making it feel crowded or narrow.

REDO THE WALLS AND CEILING

The nursery has a stunning tray ceiling, which we wanted to highlight. We chose to wallpaper with different patterns to bring in more color and texture. Too much of either pattern would have felt overwhelming, but combining the two kept things interesting.

The purple wallpaper looks like something from the 1970s—it's somewhat psychedelic. We toned it down with the intricate blue-and-green paper, which came from Secondhand Rose, a vintage wallpaper store in Manhattan. It carries more than five thousand patterns that date as far back as the 1880s, which makes it feel more like a museum than a store.

ASK THE EXPERT
SUZANNE LIPSCHUTZ

We asked Suzanne Lipschutz, the owner of Secondhand Rose, a few questions about vintage wallpaper.

Q: How/where do you find your wallpaper?
A: I've been collecting antique wallpaper for forty years. Most of my papers are American, so I have been to every state to find them. Each acquisition has its own story. Usually it's found in a building that was built no later than 1940. Paper was stocked by hardware stores and local general stores—not like today, where you have to order it. In the 1920s and '30s, wallpaper was a very cheap way of modernizing your home.

Q: Any great stories?
A: They're all great stories. I once bought a whole building in Michigan just to get the paper in the basement. It was cheaper and faster to buy the building.

Q: What are the challenges of vintage paper?
A: Depends on the age. Early papers are on newsprint, and often are dry. I keep humidifiers running twenty-four hours here. I always advise using a professional wallpaper hanger. I personally hang all papers to test them. I can hang anything!

THE PALE GREEN PAINT IS BRIGHT ENOUGH FOR A BABY'S ROOM, CLASSIC ENOUGH FOR A GUEST ROOM.

BLACKOUT
SHADES ARE
A MUST IN A
NURSERY.

WOODEN BLOCKS
ALWAYS LOOK
GREAT.

A KID'S ROOM
DOESN'T
HAVE TO
HAVE KID
ART.

STEP 2

SELECT WINDOW TREATMENTS AND ARTWORK

The deep-blue, flat roman shades complement the paint and show-case the prewar moldings around the windows, which would have been covered over had we chosen to go with drapes.

The three shadow boxes above the crib are by artist Han Xu. *We Are So Good Together* is a print by artist Dylan Fareed that we purchased from 20 × 200. It's perfect for a nursery, as it brings a sweet feeling to the room without being overly sappy. The *Unseen Forces* print was something the Hallers already owned but had in storage. We had it framed and hung it above the changing table—it plays nicely above the striped changing pad.

THIS DWR DAYBED WAS REUPHOLSTERED.

THE GREEN BOLSTER WAS CUSTOM MADE.

The Hallers needed a full nursery's worth of furnishings.

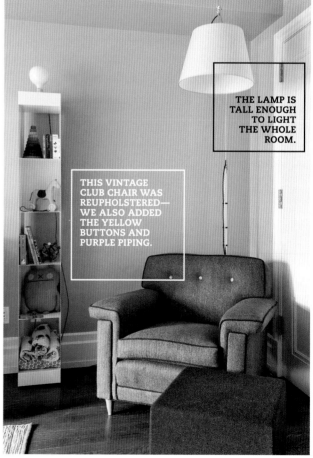

THE LAMP IS TALL ENOUGH TO LIGHT THE WHOLE ROOM.

THIS VINTAGE CLUB CHAIR WAS REUPHOLSTERED—WE ALSO ADDED THE YELLOW BUTTONS AND PURPLE PIPING.

STEP 3

FIND MULTIFUNCTIONAL FURNITURE

The Hallers needed a full nursery's worth of furnishings and gear, including a crib, a changing table, a mobile, and a chair for Mom and Dad. And because this was part guest room, they also needed a bed. A large bed would take up too much space and overcrowd the room, especially while it was still being used as a nursery. We found the sofa bed at Design Within Reach. It can lie flat as a queen-sized bed or convert into a daybed or two twin beds. We had the bolster reupholstered in purple and added the navy piping.

TOYS ADD GREAT COLOR.

ADD THE BABY FURNITURE

We chose the simple wood dresser with white drawers because it has a sharp, clean look and holds a changing pad for now—but it can be removed to leave a nice-looking dresser. Later, when the baby moves into Griffin's room, it can move with him, or it can stay in the guest room for extra storage. The gray-and-white-striped pad is colorful and has a sweetness that works in a baby's room. The crib, too, is simple and sleek—the bedding and toys are what soften it up.

THIS MOBILE IS FELT AND LEATHER AND COMES FROM ACORN IN BROOKLYN.

SHARP AND CLEAN-LOOKING

THE RUG PULLS TOGETHER ALL THE COLORS IN THE ROOM.

WALLPAPER FROM
THE WALLPAPER
COLLECTIVE

RETHINK GRIFFIN'S ROOM

The room was lacking color, organization, a work space/desk, and lighting, and the furnishings were sparse: a bed and a bookshelf.

Kids' rooms are fantastic places to take risks with bold colors and wallpaper designs. The animal wallpaper came from The Wallpaper Collective—it's especially fun because it's printed so that the animals' skeletons show up over the silhouettes, but only when the room is light, so it's not scary for kids at night.

Griffin's bed turned out to be the bottom half of a bunk bed set. We found the other half in storage and put it back together, so that when the baby is old enough, he can easily move in with his brother. We purchased a second mattress at Ikea and found the blue gingham bedding at The Land of Nod. Kids' bedding can be bold and youthful yet still have a sophisticated and stylish look to it.

TRUNKS ARE
PERFECT
FOR STORING
TOYS.

THE BRIGHT BLUE PAINT BRIGHTENS UP THE SPACE WITHOUT OVERWHELMING IT. IT'S ALSO A GREAT SHOWCASE FOR EVERYTHING ELSE.

MADE BY ARTIST SEAN KENNEY

GINGHAM BEDDING IS CLASSIC AND CUTE.

Kids' rooms are fantastic places to take risks.

ALL KIDS SHOULD HAVE THEIR OWN WORK/PLAY SPACE.

CUSTOMIZE ANY STORE-BOUGHT DESK WITH FUNKY, UNIQUE, OR VINTAGE KNOBS.

ADD SHELVING AND A WORK SPACE TO GRIFFIN'S ROOM

The Hallers asked us to create a small workstation for Griffin so that he would have a place to play games, color, and draw. We brought in a simple white activity table and replaced the knobs with a colorful set from Anthropologie. We attached the white paper roll on top so that he could easily draw, tear off the paper, and start on something else. The red lamp on top of the desk was made completely out of Lego bricks by artist Sean Kenney. It's fun and brings color to the desk, as well as more light to the room.

We replaced the white, boxy shelving unit with green metal shelves. They add color to the space and do a much better job of showcasing the books and toys than the existing shelves did. The baskets below keep all of Griffin's small toys neat and organized and also make them easy to get to. The teepee next to the shelves came from The Land of Nod, and the "A to Z" rug is one of our own designs.

A GREAT PLACE TO DISPLAY COLLECTIONS

THIS IS FROM CB2.

ELEPHANTS BRING GOOD LUCK

A FANTASTIC PLACE TO HIDE OUT

THE "A TO Z" RUG IS OUR OWN DESIGN— IT'S ROBERT'S FATHER'S HANDWRITING!

FUNCTIONAL
AND
UNOBTRUSIVE

WHERE WE ENDED

Through careful consideration of color and layout, we came up with a flexible design that can be nursery one day and guest room the next—but we have a feeling that with Griffin's fun new room, his baby brother will be asking to join him as soon as he can talk.

TAKE AWAY THE CRIB AND THE CHANGING TABLE, AND YOU HAVE AN INSTANT GUEST ROOM.

THE CARROT SEED

HOW TO

BUILD A LAMP WITH LEGO BRICKS

The Lego pieces in this lamp are built around a simple lighting fixture sourced from a discount furniture store. Artist Sean Kenney explains how to make your own lamp.

1. Start by drawing a "footprint" on graph paper, tracing a shape along the grid of the graph. This will be the top-down blueprint for the first rows of your lamp. Build the first row by placing your Lego pieces on or around the flat base of the real lamp.

2. Build a second row, exactly the same shape as the first, making sure you overlap all the pieces in the first row. This creates a solid, sturdy base on which you can continue upward.

3. Keep going, row after row, adding whatever shapes and features you'd like. As you approach the socket of the lamp, make sure you leave space for the lampshade and for any switches, pull chains, or other functional elements. Also make sure to keep the Lego pieces far enough from the lightbulb so that they won't get too hot.

4. Above all, have fun! Your lamp can take the shape of a traditional lighting fixture, or you can go wild and add windows, faces, space docks, or whatever else you'd like.

BUDGET ANALYSIS

CONTRACTOR FEES	$4,023.65
PAINT AND WALLPAPER	$1,765.19
FLOORING AND CARPETS	GIFTS
WINDOW TREATMENTS	$1,034.31
LIGHTING	$1,430.74
FURNITURE	$5,187.91
FABRIC AND UPHOLSTERY	$1,844.00
MATTRESSES AND BEDDING	$950.70
TEEPEE	$159.00
ART	$1,397.16
ACCESSORIES	$641.80
TOYS	$420.38
TOTAL	**$18,854.84**

Seaside Cabana

In the fall of 2010, we met a couple with two young kids who were in the process of building a new home in a secluded neighborhood in Palm Beach, Florida. There was a small seaside cabana on the property that needed an overhaul. It was a one-room, one-bathroom, all-white space that was located 200 yards from the main house. It had great bones but was completely lacking in charm, style, and modern comforts.

The clients asked us to work in collaboration with their architect to create a multifunctional family space. They wanted it to be sophisticated but also rustic and casual. The cabana was going to serve many functions—a place for the family to hang out and watch movies, play games, and spend days at the beach together;

WHERE WE STARTED

THE BUDGET
$25,000

THE GOAL
To design a chic, multifunctional indoor/outdoor space the entire family could enjoy

THE CLIENTS' WISH LIST

1. A fully functional kitchen/bar
2. An entertainment area
3. Vintage features and antiques
4. Natural elements throughout
5. A changing area

EVERYTHING HAD TO GO.

THE BAR/ISLAND WAS LACKING ALL OF THE ESSENTIALS— A SINK, A FREEZER, A REFRIGERATOR, AND A DISHWASHER.

The interior looked like a storage unit.

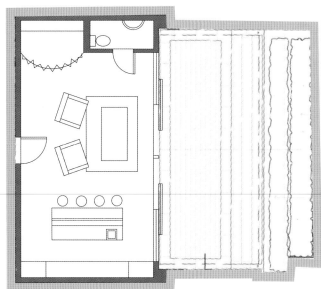

THE CABANA WAS SMALL BUT THE LAYOUT WAS OPEN.

a place for gatherings and entertaining friends; and a place to escape to, read books, and relax. They asked us to replace the bar and kitchen island with a fully functioning bar—sink and fridge included—and to create a TV area, a changing space, and an outdoor space that would serve as an extension of the inside.

Our plan was to design a functional space with a bohemian-chic vibe that combined natural elements with vintage antiques and artifacts throughout. We didn't want it to be too precious, but rather easy, open, and casual. It also needed to be durable because of its proximity to the ocean and the salty air.

The cabana was small—450 square feet—but the layout was open, with high ceilings and spectacular ocean views. So aside from the size issue, we had a lot to work with. The danger of creating multi-functional spaces in small areas is that they can end up overcrowded or cluttered, or feeling chopped up into a cluster of minispaces. But the location made our job much easier; all the outdoor private space was basically an enormous extension of the inside.

When we first came to see the cabana, our clients had just recently purchased the property, so it was essentially in the condition in which the previous owners had left it. The interior looked and felt more like a storage unit than a seaside cabana. It was stark white, with laundry-room-like tiled floors, and had basically served as an oversized closet for the family's beach supplies: grill, chairs, surfboards, coolers, and anything else that came in handy for a day in the sun. Everything had to go—the bar, the island, the floors, and the interior and exterior doors. This left us with an empty white box that had enormous potential.

REDO THE WALLS, DOORS, AND FLOORS

The architects took care of all building and construction while we focused on the interior design. They replaced the sliding doors with heavier wood-framed glass doors, covered the white ceiling in reclaimed wood, installed a new bar and kitchen island, and laid vintage Moroccan tile throughout. The place was completely transformed.

The natural woods used on the bar and countertop bring the outside in without making the cabana feel too theme-y or nautical. The Moroccan tiles that cover the floors and the bathroom walls provide color and pattern that carry through the whole space.

The place was completely transformed.

REPURPOSED AS A SINK, THIS ANTIQUE PIECE WAS ORIGINALLY A FRENCH GARDEN FOUNTAIN.

DESIGN THE BATHROOM

The existing bathroom was a small white box. Vintage Moroccan tiles gave it an exotic look and tons of character. We found the French antique sink—which was once a garden fountain—at Truetiques. We added new plumbing and a new wall-mounted faucet from Herbeau. All together, they make the space romantic and unique. The white candles and wicker basket under the sink are simple but bring a quiet elegance to the space.

ASK THE EXPERT
BENS BEN

We asked Bens Ben, the president of Mosaic House Moroccan Imports, to give us a few pointers on finding, buying, and installing great vintage tile.

Q: Could you give us some tips for choosing and using Moroccan tile?

A: Select the design before you pick the color(s). Any design can be customized to work with any color or combination of colors. Even complex designs can be made to look sleek and contemporary through color. Color and pattern help to set the tone of the room. It is important to consider whether the overall look desired is modern or traditional, classic or contemporary.

Q: What areas are best for laying tile?

A: The kitchen floor and backsplash, bathrooms, foyers, sunrooms, fireplaces, and pool areas.

Q: What types of tile are best for the kitchen?

A: I recommend using glazed mosaic tiles on areas like the kitchen backsplash, as it is a maintenance-free tile. Cement tile is composed of marble powder, cement, and natural pigments, and it is recommended that the tile be sealed for easy maintenance. While not recommended for the backsplash, it lends itself well to virtually any application.

Q: Why should people use Moroccan tile?

A: Great tile is timeless, not trendy. Handmade in Morocco as it has been for centuries, it adds depth to the overall design of the space. Its time-tested durability makes it well suited to both wet and dry spaces. Its earthiness is a calming and grounding addition to any space, and one that is easy to live with.

STEP 3

DESIGN THE BAR

The existing bar was really just a crowded countertop with glass shelves above and shuttered storage beneath. It lacked a sink, a refrigerator, and an ice maker. So unless someone was craving warm tequila, not many drinks were being served.

Switching things around and turning what had been the kitchen island into a functional wet bar with refrigeration allowed the counter-top and shelves to serve as storage. Both the bar and the countertop are built from reclaimed natural woods, which bring in a warmth and richness that had been missing before.

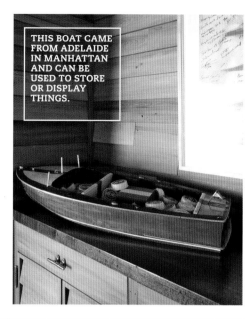

THIS BOAT CAME FROM ADELAIDE IN MANHATTAN AND CAN BE USED TO STORE OR DISPLAY THINGS.

THE ANTIQUE DRIFTWOOD CHANDELIER IS ONE OF A KIND AND CAME FROM EUROPE.

THE MIRRORS ADD BOTH FUNCTION AND CHARACTER.

RECONCEIVE THE CHANGING AREA

We needed to make this space more functional and efficient while maintaining the look that we wanted.

The existing changing room had been covered with shuttered white doors that took up too much room, so they were replaced with a curtain on a curved rod. The rod extends out of the area and adds a few more feet to move around in but doesn't take up nearly as much space as doors. The curtain is made out of vintage linen with a subtle coral print.

The built-in shelves are made from the same reclaimed wood that is used throughout the cabana. They're perfect for storing beach towels, clothing, and swim gear.

SIMPLE IS BEST—JUST ADD WHITE CANDLES AND A SMALL COLLECTION OF SHELLS.

DEFINE A SEATING AREA

The goal here was simple: cozy and functional but chic.

Because the ocean is the focal point and highlight of the space, we wanted to keep the decor simple, with a few great pieces, including the Randall Mesdon surfboard photograph that hangs above the chairs. It gives the seating area an old-school surfer vibe without overwhelming the space.

We hung the flat-screen TV above the bar so that the chairs can be turned to face it for nighttime movie watching but also so that it can be seen from the deck during outdoor gatherings.

We found the custom driftwood chandelier by Sarlo on 1stdibs. It lights up the seating area at night, and the driftwood gives the space the ultimate beachy, elegant feel.

THIS VINTAGE ZENITH RADIO STILL WORKS

THE ANTIQUE
WOOD AND METAL
COFFEE TABLE
BRINGS IN A TOUCH
OF RUSTICITY.

FINISH THE GREAT OUTDOORS

On average, it's sunny 235 days a year in Palm Beach, so the outdoor space was truly an extension of the cabana. The custom banquette on the deck serves as a great spot for watching sports or movies outside and people-watching on the beach below. All of the outdoor furniture came from Dedon. We used custom pillows and cushions for the banquette, daybeds, chairs, and chaises. They are all made from French fabrics that we found at Les Toiles Du Soleil. Some of the daybeds have canopies, offering shade for those sunny Florida days.

We used custom pillows and cushions.

ASK THE EXPERT
CAROLYN QUARTERMAINE

We asked artist and textile designer Carolyn
Quartermaine to give us some insight on the use of
vintage fabrics.

Q: Where do your vintage fabrics come from?

A: I find them at auctions in London and France, at
markets, and from dealers. The first came from my own
grandmother in Switzerland; they had been handwoven
by my great-grandmothers, collected, and handed down.
Fabrics by artists follow a long tradition. It would be
wonderful to see more fabrics that are unique one-offs
used well. I think of them as paintings on furniture or
simply hung like artwork.

Q: Why is it important to use unique fabrics?

A: A true identity is imperative in a world of mass
production and copies. A wonderful hand-painted fabric is
like a dress by the best designer. It adds sparkle to a room.
It's an investment piece.

Q: Where do you get inspired?

A: I see beauty in most things and most places. It's an
attitude and a way of living. I love the sea, I love fields of
flowers, but inspiration is more from within than a visual.

Q: Can you tell us about the screen-printing process?

A: A screen is held in your hands and placed on the
cloth, and then you push the ink through with a squeegee
to make an impression. It's a process that can be as
perfect and exact or as random as you wish.

WHERE WE ENDED

We incorporated raw woods and natural elements with vintage furnishings and decor, giving the space a bohemian chic beach look and allowing it to serve many different functions.

THE FLAT-SCREEN IS LARGE BUT DOESN'T TAKE OVER.

WHITE WALLS MAKE A GREAT CANVAS FOR COLORFUL FURNISHINGS.

THE CURVED CURTAIN ROD GIVES SOME EXTRA ROOM FOR CHANGING BUT KEEPS THE SPACE OPEN.

HOW TO

INCORPORATE VINTAGE PLUMBING FIXTURES

1.
LOOK FOR VINTAGE PLUMBING FIXTURES ON SITES LIKE TRUETIQUES, EBAY, ETSY, AND 1STDIBS, AS WELL AS IN ANTIQUES STORES AND AT FLEA MARKETS.

2.
BE IMAGINATIVE. SOMETHING THAT WAS ORIGINALLY A FOUNTAIN CAN BE REPURPOSED AS A POWDER-ROOM SINK WITH MODERN PLUMBING AND FAUCETS.

3.
TALK TO YOUR PLUMBER AND MAKE SURE THAT HE OR SHE WILL BE ABLE TO HOOK THE SINK UP TO YOUR EXISTING PIPES.

4.
PURCHASE NEW FAUCETS TO GO WITH THE VINTAGE SINK. (WITH AN ANTIQUE FRENCH FOUNTAIN WALL SINK YOU WILL NEED A WALL-MOUNTED "TAP" FAUCET.)

BUDGET ANALYSIS

"FAMILY" RUG	GIFT
LIGHTING	$2,179.00
PLUMBING FIXTURES	$3,011.60
SINK	$704.90
FURNITURE	$6,681.76
CUSTOM CHANGING-ROOM CURTAIN	$595.29
SURFBOARD PHOTO	$5,860.00
ACCESSORIES	$3,987.70
MISCELLANEOUS	$106.19
TOTAL	$23,126.44

SOURCES

A

APPLIANCES AND KITCHENWARE

BARI RESTAURANT SUPPLY
240 Bowery
New York, NY 10012
(212) 925-3845
www.bariequipment.com

BLUE STAR
www.bluestarcooking.com

BOWERY RESTAURANT SUPPLY
183 Bowery
New York, NY 10002
(212) 254-9720

GRINGER AND SONS
www.gringerandsons.com

HERBEAU
(800) 547-1608
www.herbeau.com

KRUP'S KITCHEN AND BATH
11 West 18th Street
New York, NY 10011
(212) 243-5787
www.krupskitchenandbath.net

SMOLKA
www.smolka.biz

WHISK
231 Bedford Avenue
Brooklyn, NY 11211
(718) 218-7230
www.whisknyc.com

ARCHIVAL, ART, AND CRAFT SUPPLIES

A. I. FRIEDMAN
(800) 204-6352
www.aifriedman.com

ASHLEY DISTRIBUTORS
(323) 937-2669
www.ashleydistributors.com

BEAD MERCHANT
www.beadmerchant.com

BROOKLYN GENERAL STORE
www.brooklyngeneral.com

DICK BLICK
(800) 828-4548
www.dickblick.com

HOBBY LOBBY
www.hobbylobby.com

ART, ARTISTS, AND GALLERIES

20 × 200
(212) 219-0166
www.20x200.com

PATRICK CARIOU
www.patrickcariou.com

ANN CARRINGTON
www.anncarrington.co.uk

CLIC
255 Centre Street
New York, NY 10013
(212) 966-2766
www.clicgallery.com

HEIDI CODY
www.heidicody.com

MARC DENNIS
www.marcdennis.com

JAN ELENI
www.janeleni.com

EXHIBITION A
www.exhibitiona.com

BRIAN FINKE
www.brianfinke.com

GAGOSIAN GALLERY
www.gagosian.com

HALF GALLERY
208 Forsyth Street
New York, NY 10002
www.halfgallery.com

HARRIS LIEBERMAN GALLERY
508 West 26th Street
New York, NY 10011
(212) 206-1290
www.harrislieberman.com

SEAN KENNEY
www.seankenney.com

HASTED KRAEUTLER
537 West 24th Street
New York, NY 10011
(212) 627-0006
www.hastedkraeutler.com

KNOX MARTIN
www.knoxmartin.com

LINDA MASON
www.lindamason.com

RANDALL MESDON
www.clicgallery.com/artists/randall-mesdon/index.htm

ROOM 125
www.room125nyc.com

TERRY ROSEN
www.terryrosen.com

JAMES SEWARD
www.jameslseward.com

MATT SIREN
www.mattsiren.com

GUSTAVO TEN HOEVER
www.gthstudio.com

WOODWARD GALLERY
133 Eldridge Street
New York, NY 10002
(212) 966-3411
www.woodwardgallery.net

YANCEY RICHARDSON GALLERY
535 West 22nd Street, 3rd floor
New York, NY 10011
(646) 230-9610
www.yanceyrichardson.com

YELLOW FEVER CREATIVE
www.yellowfever
creative.com

ARTISANS
JOHN HOUSHMAND
www.johnhoushmand.com

GAETANO PESCE
www.gaetanopesce.com

POESIS
www.poesisdesign.com

C

CARPET TILE
FLOR
(866) 952-4093
www.flor.com

CLOSET SYSTEMS
CALIFORNIA CLOSETS
(866) 861-5887
www.californiaclosets.com

F

FABRIC, TRIM, AND UPHOLSTERY
B&J FABRICS
525 Seventh Avenue
New York, NY 10018
(212) 354-8150
www.bandjfabrics.com

BETTERTEX
450 Broadway, 2nd floor
New York, NY 10013
(212) 431-3373
www.bettertex.com

DMD INTERIOR DISCOUNT FABRIC TRIM AND WALLCOVERING
2 Denise Drive
Patchogue, NY 11772
(631) 627-3787

M&J TRIMMING
1008 Sixth Avenue
New York, NY 10018
(212) 391-6200
www.mjtrim.com

MAHARAM
(800) 645-3943
www.maharam.com

MOOD DESIGNER FABRIC
www.moodfabrics.com

FRAMING
ALLERTON CUSTOM FRAMING
241 Eighth Avenue
New York, NY 10011
(646) 486-3781
www.allertoncustom
framing.com

G

GLASS AND MIRRORS
AAA GLASS AND MIRROR
4205 South Sepulveda Boulevard
Culver City, CA 90230
(310) 314-5277
www.aaaglassandmirror.com

ALLSTATE GLASS
85 Kenmare Street
New York, NY 10012
(212) 226-2517
www.allstateglasscorp.com

H

HOME FURNISHINGS— ANTIQUE/ HANDMADE/ VINTAGE
ADELAIDE
702 Greenwich Street
New York, NY 10014
(212) 627-0508
www.adelaideny.com

ANTIQUE EMPORIUM OF ASBURY PARK
646 Cookman Avenue
Asbury Park, NJ 07712
(732) 774-8230
www.antiqueemporium
ofasburypark.com

ANTIQUE NV
102 South First Street
Jenks, OK 74037
(918) 298-5962
www.antiquenv.com

BOOTSNGUS
www.etsy.com/shop/
bootsngus

BRIGHT LYONS
383 Atlantic Avenue
Brooklyn, NY 11217
(718) 855-5463
www.brightlyons.com

CITY FOUNDRY
365 Atlantic Avenue
Brooklyn, NY 11217
(718) 923-1786
www.cityfoundry.com

CLEVELAND ART
www.clevelandart.com

DARR
369 Atlantic Avenue
Brooklyn, NY 11217
(718) 797-9733
www.shopdarr.com

DISPELA ANTIQUES
459 South La Brea Avenue
Los Angeles, CA 90036
(323) 934-9939
www.dispelaantiques.com

THE ECLECTIC SHOCK
www.etsy.com/shop/theeclecticshock

ESTATE ECLECTIC
www.etsy.com/shop/estateeclectic

ETSY
www.etsy.com

1STDIBS
www.1stdibs.com

THE FRAYED KNOT
601 Newark Street
Hoboken, NJ 07030
(917) 854-5945
www.thefrayedknotonline.com

FS20
647 Cookman Avenue
Asbury Park, NJ 07712
(732) 502-8999
www.fs20.com

FURBISH STUDIO
312 West Johnson Street
Raleigh, NC 27603
(919) 521-4981
www.furbishstudio.com

THE FUTURE PERFECT
www.thefutureperfect.com

HOLLER & SQUALL
119 Atlantic Avenue
Brooklyn, NY 11201
(347) 223-4685
www.hollerandsquall.com

HORSEMAN ANTIQUES
351 Atlantic Avenue
Brooklyn, NY 11217
(718) 596-1048
www.horsemanantiques.net

HOUSING WORKS
www.housingworks.org

JUNK
motherofjunk2.
blogspot.com

KIOSK
www.kioskkiosk.com

THE LIVELY SET
33 Bedford Street
New York, NY 10014
(212) 807-8417

LOST CITY ARTS
18 Cooper Square
New York, NY 10003
(212) 375-0500
www.lostcityarts.com

MAIN STREET JUNCTION
103 East Main Street
Jenks, OK 74037
(918) 296-7005

MALEKAN RUGS AND ANTIQUES
3635 South Dixie Highway
West Palm Beach, FL 33405
(561) 833-6194

MANTIQUES MODERN
146 West 22nd Street
New York, NY 10011
(212) 206-1494
www.mantiquesmodern.com

**MEEKER AVENUE
VINTAGE
AND ANTIQUES**
391 Leonard Street
Brooklyn, NY 11211
(718) 302- 3532
www.meekerantiques.com

**MISS MCGILLICUTTY'S
ANTIQUES**
106 East Main Street
Jenks, OK 74037
(918) 298-7997
www.missmcgillicuttys
antiques.com

**MOON RIVER
CHATTEL**
62 Grand Street
Brooklyn, NY 11211
(718) 388-1121
www.moonriverchattel.com

OLDE GOODE THINGS
(888) 233-9678
www.ogtstore.com

PAULA RUBENSTEIN
21 Bond Street
New York, NY 10012
(212) 966-8954

THE PIER ANTIQUES SHOW
www.stellashows.com

RED MODERN
www.redmodernfurniture.com

REGAN AND SMITH
602 Warren Street
Hudson, NY 12534
(917) 757-5310
www.reganandsmith.com

RE*POP
www.repopny.com

RIVER CITY TRADING POST
301 East Main Street
Jenks, OK 74037
(918) 299-5998
www.facebook.com/pages/
river-city-trading-
post/128001817212558

SANTA MONICA FLEA MARKET
(323) 933-2511
www.santamonicaairport
antiquemarket.com

SIT AND READ FURNITURE
www.sit-read.com

STELLA DALLAS
218 Thompson Street
New York, NY 10012
(212) 674-0447

SUNDAY LOVE
624 Grand Street
Brooklyn, NY 11211
(347) 457-5453
www.sundaylove.biz

TINI
515 South Fairfax Avenue
Los Angeles, CA 90036
(323) 938-9230
www.thisisnotikea.com

A TREE GROWS IN BROOKLYN
479 Grand Street
Brooklyn, NY 11211
(347) 752-2911

TRUETIQUES
www.truetiques.com/servlet/
StoreFront

TWO JAKES
320 Wythe Avenue
Brooklyn, NY 11211
(718) 782-7780
www.twojakes.com

HOME FURNISHINGS— CONTEMPORARY

ABC CARPET AND HOME
www.abchome.com

ANTHROPOLOGIE
(800) 309-2500
www.anthropologie.com

AREAWARE
www.areaware.com

BED BATH AND BEYOND
(800) 462-3966
www.bedbathandbeyond.com

BEND SEATING
www.bendseating.com

BLU DOT
www.bludot.com

BRAHMS MOUNT
(800) 545-9347
www.brahmsmount.com

CALYPSO ST. BARTH
(866) 422-5977
www.calypsostbarth.com

FERNANDO AND HUMBERTO CAMPANA
www.campanas.com.br

CANVAS
www.shop.canvashomestore.com

CAPPELLINI
www.cappellini.it

CB2
(800) 606-6252
www.cb2.com

THE CONRAN SHOP
(866) 755-9079
www.conranusa.com

THE CONTAINER STORE
(888) 266-8246
www.containerstore.com

CRATE AND BARREL
(800) 967-6696
www.crateandbarrel.com

C WONDER
(855) 896-6337
www.cwonder.com

DESIGN WITHIN REACH
(800) 944-2233
www.dwr.com

EDIT
Center 1
3524C South Peoria
Tulsa, OK 74105
(918) 747-7477
www.edittulsa.com

GREENHOUSE
(866) 575-4437
www.greenhousedesignstudio.com

HAUS INTERIOR
www.hausinterior.com

HOME INFATUATION
(877) 224-8925
www.homeinfatuation.com

HOMEGOODS
(800) 888-0776
www.homegoods.com

HORNE
(877) 404-6763
www.shophorne.com

IKEA
www.ikea.com

JONATHAN ADLER
(800) 963-0891
www.jonathanadler.com

KARTELL
www.kartell.com

THE LAND OF NOD
(800) 933-9904
www.landofnod.com

LAYLA
86 Hoyt Street
Brooklyn, NY 11201
(718) 222-1933
www.layla-bklyn.com

**LES TOILES
DU SOLEIL**
261 West 19th Street
New York, NY 10011
(212) 229-4730
www.lestoilesdusoleilnyc.com

LILLIAN AUGUST
www.lillianaugust.com

LOOPEE DESIGN
(877) 728-9601
www.loopeedesign.com

MARSHALLS
(800) 627-7425
www.marshallsonline.com

MATTER
405 Broome Street
New York, NY 10013
(212) 343-2160
www.mattermatters.com

MC&CO
57 North 6th Street
Brooklyn, NY 11211
(718) 388-3551
www.mcandco.us

THE MEAT HOOK
100 Frost Street
Brooklyn, NY 11211
(718) 349-5033
www. the-meathook.com

MODANI
www.modani.com

**MOMA DESIGN
STORE**
(800) 851-4509
www.momastore.org

MUJI
www.muji.us

NJ MODERN
www.njmodern.com

O & G STUDIO
www.oandgstudio.com

PIER 1 IMPORTS
(800) 245-4595
www.pier1.com

PROPERTY
14 Wooster Street
New York, NY 10013
(917) 237-0123
www.property
furniture.com

**RESTORATION
HARDWARE**
(800) 910-9836
www.restoration
hardware.com

**ROOM
AND BOARD**
(800) 301-9720
www.roomandboard.com

S. R. HUGHES
Center 1
3410 South Peoria,
 Suite 100
Tulsa, OK 74105
(918) 742-5515
www.srhughes.com

SPROUT HOME
www.sprouthome.com

T. A. LORTON
1343 East 15th Street
Tulsa, OK 74120
(918) 743-1600
www.talorton.com

THOMAS SIRES
243 Elizabeth Street
New York, NY 10012
(646) 692-4472
www.thomassires.com

TREASURE & BOND
350 West Broadway
New York, NY 10013
(646) 669-9049
www.treasureand
bond.com

**URBAN
OUTFITTERS**
(800) 282-2200
www.urbanoutfitters.com

VINTAGE MODERN
(800) 618-2960
www.vandm.com

VITRA
29 Ninth Avenue
New York, NY 10014
(212) 463-5750
www.vitra.com

WEST ELM
(888) 922-4119
www.westelm.com

WOLF HOME
www.wolfhomeny.com

Z GALLERIE
(800) 908-6748
www.zgallerie.com

HOME IMPROVEMENT

DO-IT-CENTER
www.doitcenter.com

THE HOME DEPOT
(800) 466-3337
www.homedepot.com

L

LIGHTING

BOWERY LIGHTING CO.
1210 Broadhollow Road
East Farmingdale, NY 11735
(866) 744-5166
www.bowerylights.com

CANAL LIGHTING AND PARTS
313 Canal Street
New York, NY 10013
(212) 343-0218

DUNES AND DUCHESS
www.dunesandduchess.com

JUST SHADES
21 Spring Street
New York, NY 10012
(212) 966-2757
www.justshadesny.com

LITE MAKERS
(718) 729-7700
www.litemakers.com

NUD COLLECTION
www.nudcollection.com

**P. W. VINTAGE
LIGHTING**
2 State Road
Great Barrington, MA 01230
(866) 561-3158
www.pwvintagelighting.com

SAFETYBULBS.COM
(856) 427-9411
www.safetybulbs.com

SARLO
(415) 863-1001
www.gabriellasarlo.com

YLIGHTING
(866) 428-9289
www.ylighting.com

M

MISCELLANEOUS

2JANE.COM
(888) 667-6961
www.2jane.com

**BEETHOVEN
PIANOS**
232 West 58th Street
New York, NY 10019
(800) 241-0001 or
(212) 765-7300
www.beethoven
pianos.com

**DISTRICT
DOG**
www.districtdog.com

**DOUG'S WORD
CLOCKS**
www.dougswordclocks.com

**ECONOMY
FOAM + FUTONS**
56 West 8th Street
New York, NY 10011
(212) 475-4800
www.economyfoam
andfutons.com

ECOSMART FIRE
(888) 590-3335
www.ecosmartfire.com

FASTSIGNS
www.fastsigns.com

GREEN TIRE BIKE SHOP
www.greentirebikes.com

PS9 PET SUPPLIES
169 North 9th Street
Brooklyn, NY 11211
(718) 486-6465
www.ps9pets.com

**SMC STONE
INTERNATIONAL INC.**
640 Morgan Avenue
Brooklyn, NY 11222
(718) 599-2999
www.smcstone.com

P

PAINT
BENJAMIN MOORE
(855) 724-6802
www.benjamin
moore.com

JANOVIC
www.janovic.com

PEARL PAINT
(800) 451-7327
www.pearlpaint.com

STARK PAINT
www.starkpaint.com

Novogratz for Stark is
available at http://
www.thenovogratz.com

PHOTO SERVICES
DUGGAL
29 West 23rd Street
New York, NY 10010
(212) 242-7000

T

www.duggal.com

TILE
BELLA TILE
178 First Avenue
New York, NY 10009
(212) 475-2909
www.bellatilenyc.com

**MOSAIC HOUSE
MOROCCAN IMPORTS**
32 West 22nd Street
New York, NY 10010
(212) 414-2525
www. mosaichse.com

TOYS
ACORN
323 Atlantic Avenue
Brooklyn, NY 11201
(718) 522-3760
www. acorntoyshop.com

KIDROBOT
(877) 762-6543
www.kidrobot.com

MINKY MONKEY
588 Old Mammoth Road #4
Mammoth Lakes, CA 93546
(760) 934-1963
www.minkymonkeytoys.com

WALL GRAPHICS/
WALLPAPER
BLIK
(866) 262-2545
www.whatisblik.com

FLAVOR PAPER
216 Pacific Street
Brooklyn, NY 11201
(718) 422-0230
www.flavorpaper.com

SECONDHAND ROSE
230 Fifth Avenue,
    Suite #510
New York, NY 10001
(212) 393-9002
www.secondhandrose.com

THE WALLPAPER COLLECTIVE
www.wallpapercollective.com

WALNUT WALLPAPER
7424 Beverly Boulevard
Los Angeles, CA 90036
(323) 932-9166
www.walnutwallpaper.com

WINDOW
TREATMENTS
THE SHADE STORE
(800) 754-1455
www.theshadestore.com

ACKNOWLEDGMENTS

A huge thank-you to everyone at Artisan, especially LIA RONNEN, our editor. It's a privilege and an honor to work with someone we like and respect as much as you.

Thanks to MARK REITER, our good friend and wonderful agent.

Thanks to BONNIE SIEGLER, ANDREW CAPELLI, and KRISTEN REN of Eight and a Half, New York, for helping with the design of this book.

Thank you to the amazingly talented photographers who shot these chapters: MATTHEW WILLIAMS, TIM GEANY, SHANE BEVEL, GLENN HAYDU, JOSHUA McHUGH, COSTAS PICADOS, and ARIADNA BUFI.

Thank you to everyone at Left/Right, especially KEN, BANKS, NEIL, and DAVID, and to everyone at HGTV—especially COURTNEY WHITE.

And a ton of love and gratitude goes out to our guys: GARY, STEFAN, and RITCHIE. And, of course, to the amazing HENI and AGNES.

Last but not least, a big thank-you to our incredible design team: ALI LEVIN, ANABEL MURILLO, ELSPETH BENOIT, and JEN (WIGGA WIGGA) WEIGLE.

INDEX

ILLUSTRATION CREDITS

The authors and publisher wish to thank the following for permission to reprint their illustrations.

Shane Bevel: pp. 6 (Pioneering Attic, after), 56, 60–69. **Shane Bevel for HGTV/Scripps Networks, LLC:** pp. 6 (Pioneering Attic, before), 58.

Ariadna Bufi: pp. 6 (Tree House, both), 7 (Beach House, after), 10 (top), 100, 102 (top), 104–5, 106 (top left), 108–10, 111 (flooring and carpets, copper fixtures, furniture, mattress and linens, hammock, accessories, mosquito netting, total), 126, 129 (bottom right), 134 (top), 135 (center left; right), 139 (accessories), 246, 250–51 (center), 251 (right), 252, 253 (top), 254, 255 (all except before photo), 256, 258–59, 261 (window treatments, lighting, appliances, bathroom remodels, bar cart, light boxes, accessories, total).

Tim Geany: pp. 98, 102 (bottom), 103, 106 (right; bottom left), 107, 111 (contractor fees, window treatments, lighting, iron plate for roof).

Glenn Haydu: pp. 7 (Boutique Hotel, before), 230–31.

Left/Right, Inc. for HGTV/Scripps Networks, LLC: pp. 6 (Hipster Haven, before), 72–73.

Joshua McHugh: pp. 228, 232 (left; bottom), 233 (bottom), 236–39, 241 (bottom left); 245 (window treatments, custom woodworking, lobby, bar, lounge, game area, standard bedrooms, suites, miscellaneous).

Will Norton for HGTV/Scripps Networks, LLC: pp. 6 (Ski Condo, before), 28–29, 31 (right).

Robert and Cortney Novogratz: All floor plans; pp. 7 (Beach House, before), 248–49, 255 (top left).

Costas Picados: pp. 6 (Surf Shack, after; Dream Duplex, after), 7 (Beach Condo, after), 130, 131 (left, top and bottom), 132 (bottom), 133, 134 (bottom), 136–38, 139 (kitchen and dining table, furniture, art), 144–45 (center), 146, 147 (center; left), 148–51, 153 (flooring and carpets, lighting, fireplace, furniture, pillows, art, flowers, total), 168, 172 (right), 178 (left), 179, 181 (right), 182–83.

Emilee Ramsier for HGTV/Scripps Networks, LLC: pp. 6 (Queens Condo, before; Urban Sanctuary, before; Reader's Refuge, before; City Reserve, before; Surf Shack, before; Dream Duplex, before), 7 (Suburban Basement, before; Model Home, both; Beach Condo, before; Village Railroad, before; Triplets' Bedroom, before; Brooklyn Modern, before; Last-Minute Nursery, before), 14–15, 24, 42–43, 47, 48 (top), 50–51 (center), 51 (right), 55 (closet system and wardrobe), 86–87, 92, 114–15, 128, 129 (bottom left), 135 (top, both), 139 (window treatments, appliances, bedding), 142–43, 156–57, 159 (bottom right), 170–71, 172 (left), 173 (right), 173 (top left), 174 (bottom right), 175, 178 (bottom right), 184, 185 (contractor fees, wallpaper, lighting, bedding), 188–91, 192 (top), 193 (bottom), 194 (left), 195–98, 199 (flooring and carpets, mirror wall, bedding, electronics, art), 202–3, 207 (inset), 216, 222 (bottom right), 264–65, 278–79.

Matthew Williams: pp. 1–3, 6 (Queens Condo, after; Ski Condo, after; Urban Sanctuary, after; Hipster Haven, after; Reader's Refuge, after; City Reserve, after), 7 (Suburban Basement, after; Village Railroad, after; Triplets' Bedroom, after; Boutique Hotel, after; Brooklyn Modern, after; Last-Minute Nursery, after; Seaside Cabana, after), 8, 10 (bottom), 11–12, 16–23, 25–26, 30 (left), 30–31 (center), 32–40, 44–45, 46 (left), 48 (bottom), 49, 50 (left), 52–54, 55 (all but closet system and wardrobe), 70, 74–84, 88–91, 93–97, 112, 116–25, 131 (right), 132 (top), 139 (contractor fees, wallpaper, flooring and carpets, lighting, total), 140–41, 144 (left), 145 (top), 147 (right), 152, 153 (contractor fees, bar and bar accessories, books, vases), 154–55, 158, 159 (top right; left), 160–67, 172 (carpet tile details), 173 (bottom left), 174 (left; top right), 176–77, 180, 185 (flooring and carpets, window treatments, "Family" light boxes, furniture, art, space curtain, accessories, miscellaneous, total), 186, 193 (top), 194 (right), 199 (contractor fees, wallpaper, lighting, furniture, total), 200, 204–6, 207 (large), 208–14, 218–21, 222 (left), 223–27, 232–33 (center), 234–35, 240, 241 (right), 242–44, 245 (outdoor patio, total), 250 (left), 253 (bottom), 257, 260, 261 (contractor fees, kitchen remodel, minibar, pool table), 262, 266–76, 280–92, 296–307.

Photograph of Seaside Cabana on pages 7 (before) and 294 courtesy of the homeowners.